LANDMARK VIS

Barbados

Don Philpott

Acknowledgements

My thanks to all those who assisted me in the preparation of this guide. In particular, I would like to thank Vanessa Marti of Ruder Finn, American Airlines, the Barbados Tourism Authority, Robin Simmons of Blue Horizon and Emerson Clarke, our guide. I would also like to dedicate this book to the memory of Barbara Browne of the BTA who showed me so much kindness on previous visits to the island.

• Top Tips •

Get to know the Island

Travel by bus. A great way to meet the locals and visit the different parishes, each of which is different and has something special to offer.

Party down at the Gap

There is nowhere quite like the Gap and no trip to Barbados is complete without spending an evening or two wining, dining and dancing under the stars.

Be Adventurous

Barbados has wonderful island fare so don't be afraid to tuck into conkies, cou-cou, flying fish and souse.

Be Wild

Discover the beauty of the island's exotic flora and fauna with visits to Andromeda Gardens, Animal Flower Cave, and the Barbados Wildlife Reserve.

Dive In

Explore the exciting world beneath the waves. If you have never snorkeled or scuba-dived before, this is an idyllic place to learn.

Opposite: Morgan Lewis Mill

LANDMARK VISITORS GUIDE

Barbados

Don Philpott

• CONTENTS •

FACTFILE

INDEX 140/1

*B*arbados is a near-perfect tropical coral island surrounded by golden sands and turquoise warm waters, and with year-round sunshine. The Bajans, the island people, are genuinely warm and friendly, the scenery is stunning, the history exciting, the accommodation first class, the food excellent, and the opportunities for water and land-borne sports are enormous. What more could you ask?

GETTING THERE

By air

Grantley Adams International Airport in the south of the island, 8 miles (13km) east of Bridgetown, and is served by a number of international airlines, including American Airlines, Air Canada, Air Jamaica, British Airways, British West Indian Airways (BWIA), Caledonian, Canadian Holidays and Virgin Atlantic. There are also many charter operators flying to the island. It is one of the few locations in the world where Concorde makes scheduled stops.

From North America the main departure points are New York, Miami, Boston, Toronto and Montreal; and from Europe: London and Frankfurt.

There are also a number of regional airlines providing connecting flights and services to neighboring Caribbean Islands. These airlines include LIAT, BWIA and Air Martinique.

LIAT operates services between Barbados to Anguilla, Antigua, Caracas, Dominica, Grenada, Guadeloupe, Guyana, Martinique, Montserrat, Nevis, Port of Spain, San Juan, St Croix, St Kitts, St Lucia, St Maarten, St Thomas, St Vincent, Tobago and Tortola.

Typical flying times to Barbados

- **San Juan** 1 hour and 30 minutes
- **Miami** 3 hours and 40 minutes
- **New York** 4 hours and 20 minutes
- **Montreal** and **Toronto** 5 hours
- **Frankfurt** 9 hours
- **London** 8 hours

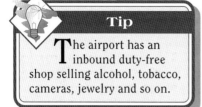

Tip

The airport has an inbound duty-free shop selling alcohol, tobacco, cameras, jewelry and so on.

Taxis are plentiful and operate on fixed prices, and there is also an airport bus service which leaves every ten minutes or so! It takes about 45 minutes to get to Bridgetown and costs Bds$1.50.

By sea

A number of major international cruise lines regularly visit the Port of Bridgetown that has become a frequent and deserved recipient of the prestigious Port of the Year Award. Around 500,000 passengers come ashore every year. The port has a modern $6 million deep-water facility about half a mile (0.8km) from the city center. Most cruise ships arrive early in the morning and sail in the evening, allowing a full day for sightseeing, shopping and relaxation. The Cruise Terminal has more than thirty duty-free shops and local vendors as well as a modern telecommunications center.

Cruise lines include: Carnival, Celebrity Cruises, Costa Cruise Line, Crystal, Cunard, Fantasy Cruises, Holland America, Norwegian Cruise Line, P&O, Princess Cruises, Radisson Seven Seas Cruises, Renaissance Cruises, Royal Caribbean, Seabourn, Silversea, Seawind, Star Clippers, Sun Cruises and Windstar.

CLOTHING AND PACKING

Light, loose and informal clothing is best. Swimwear is fine on the beach or by the pool, but cover up a little if walking around town or going for a meal. Most tourist hotels and restaurants do not have dress codes, although some prefer men to wear jackets but not ties, for dinner. Many people after spending a day on the beach like to dress up for dinner and there are no problems if you want to do this.

Tip

Get hold of your **Caribbean Classic discount card** as soon as you can. It offers substantial discounts in many restaurants, shops and attractions and car rental companies. The card which costs Bds$20 comes with a members' directory listing all the outlets which honor it, not only on Barbados but on a number of other Caribbean islands as well. The card can sometimes be obtained in advance through your travel company, or is available at the airport bureau de change and most island banks (☎ 437-3929).

An added bonus is that the names of all card holders are entered into an annual lottery with the chance of winning an all expenses-paid luxury holiday.

Some island establishments and clubs, however, still retain the rather more quaint English traditions of dressing for dinner, and insist on men wearing jackets and ties in formal areas.

Evening temperatures can dip just a little, and a sweater, light jacket or wrap can come in useful. Pack sandals for the beach as the sand can get too hot to walk on, and if you plan to go walking in the interior, take lightweight trousers and sturdy footwear. A lightweight waterproof jacket is also a good idea if you plan to go hiking, sailing or similar.

A hat, sunglasses and a good sunscreen lotion are also essential, and if you don't have a sun hat, buy a straw hat as soon as you arrive on the island because they are perfect for the job and make great souvenirs.

GEOGRAPHY

Barbados is the most easterly of the Caribbean islands. It lies 100 miles (160km) east of St Lucia in the Windward Islands, the closest island, in the southern sector of the eastern Caribbean. Miami is more than 1,600 miles (2576km) to the north-west, New York 2,000 miles (3220km) to the north, and London almost 4,200 miles (6762km) to the north-east.

The island is roughly triangular in shape, and is about 21 miles (34km) from north-west to southeast, and about 14 miles (23km) from east to west, covering a total area of about 166sq miles (431sq km). Although close to the Windward Islands, Barbados is not part of the Lesser Antilles and differs both in geological history and landscape, being less mountainous and with a less varied plant and animal life.

There is a striking contrast between the leeward west coast with its turquoise seas and white sand palm-fringed beaches, and the cliffs and white Atlantic rollers of the eastern windward coastline. Most of the land is sedimentary rock, laid down about 70 million years ago beneath the sea, and then covered with layers of chalk and coral deposits.

So, in geological terms, Barbados is still a baby. Between 750,000 and one million years ago, during a period of massive earth movement, the island was literally thrust out of the sea, and the rock layers were then tiled by enormous pressure to form the present mountains and terraces. In most places the land is still covered with a deep layer of nutrient rich coral up to 300 feet (90m) thick. The exception is in the north-east, in the area known as the **Scotland District,** where the lack of the protective coral layer, has meant much more erosion. About three-quarters of the land is arable, although only about forty per cent is under permanent cultivation.

The highest point is **Mount Hillaby** 1,115 feet (340m). To the north-east is the rugged Scotland District, to the south the land slopes to the St George Valley, the last area to emerge from the sea, which then rises to the Christ Church Ridge, about 400 feet (122m). To the west and north-west, the land slopes in a series of terraces to the sea. Coral reefs surround most of the island.

(cont'd on page 12)

BARBADOS

Brighton Beach

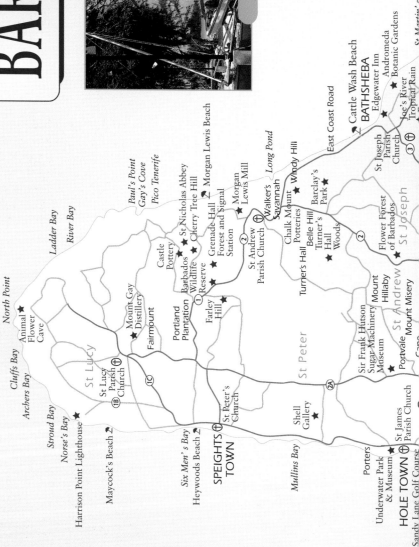

N
E
W
S

Cliffs Bay
Archers Bay
North Point

Stroud Bay
Norse's Bay
Harrison Point Lighthouse

Animal Flower Cave

Ladder Bay
River Bay

Paul's Point
Gay's Cove
Pico Tenerife

St Lucy

Mount Gay Distillery
Fairmount

Castle Pottery

St Nicholas Abbey
Cherry Tree Hill
Morgan Lewis Beach

St Lucy Parish Church
1B
1C

Portland Plantation

Barbados Wildlife Reserve
1
Farley Hill

Grenade Hall Forest and Signal Station

Morgan Lewis Mill

Long Pond

Walker's Savannah
Windy Hill

St Andrew Parish Church
2

Chalk Mount Potteries
Belle Hill
Turner's Hall Woods
Barclay's Park

Maycock's Beach

SPEIGHTS TOWN
St Peter's Church

Six Men's Bay
Heywoods Beach

St Peter

Shell Gallery

2A

Turner's Hall Woods

Sir Frank Hutson Sugar Machinery Museum
Mount Hillaby

Portvale
Mount Misery

St Andrew

Flower Forest of Barbados

St Joseph
2

Mullins Bay

Porters

Underwater Park & Museum

St James Parish Church

HOLE TOWN

Sandy Lane Golf Course

East Coast Road

Cattle Wash Beach
BATHSHEBA
Edgewater Inn
Andromeda Botanic Gardens

St Joseph Parish Church
3

Joe's River
Tropical Rain

St Martin's

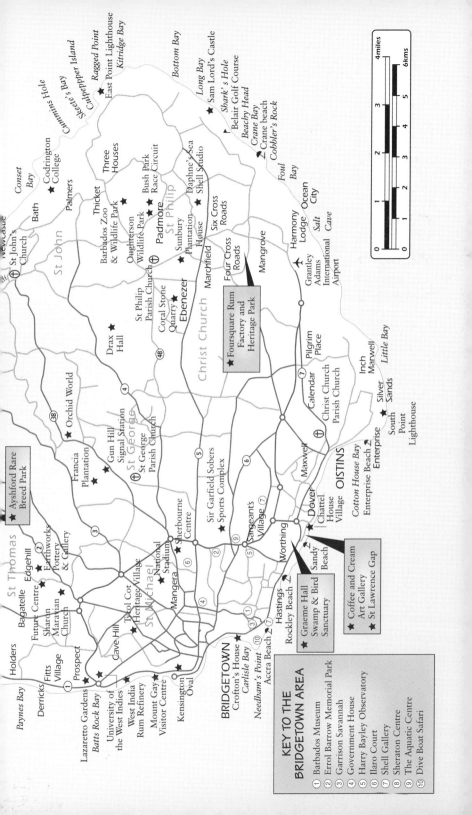

Because of the hard coral layer, rivers have not been able to carve a path through except in the Scotland District, and most rainfall permeates through the limestone into underground streams and springs which are tapped to provide most of the island's drinking water.

HISTORY

Recent excavations have found that there was a permanent settlement on Barbados as far back as 1630 BC and some of the finds have attracted international interest. What was first thought to have been simply several piles of pots stacked on top of each other is now believed to have been a water well. Whatever happened to these original settlers is not known but it does shatter the theory that the first to arrive on the island were Amerindians who came in their dug-out canoes from the Orinoco region of South America.

The Amerindians

It is not known when the Amerindians first arrived, but it is believed to have been about AD 500 – 2,000 years after the original settlers. Little is known about their life on the island other than that they were peaceful farmers and fishermen, but they had certainly disappeared by the time the first English settlers arrived. Almost certainly they were followed by Arawak Amerindians who introduced many of their customs and crafts, such as boat building, weaving and pottery. They were such skilled weavers, that they could make baskets from strips of leaves which were completely watertight.

The Arawaks lived in small settlements usually close to the sea and with small clearings inland where they grew basic crops.

The Caribs

They were ousted by the warlike Caribs who migrated north along the same route around 1200 AD. It is known that the Caribs had a well developed social system and common language throughout the islands. They were led by hereditary kings called 'caciques', while 'shamans' were the religious leaders. Their reputation as warriors was fearsome, and their war canoes could hold more than a hundred men able to paddle fast enough to catch a sailing ship.

Cannibalism

They were feared by Europeans because of horrific stories about cannibalism with victims being roasted on spits. The Caribs were even said to have a taste preference, thinking Frenchmen were the most tasty, and then the English and Dutch, with the Spanish considered stringy and almost inedible. They get their name from the Spanish word 'caribal' which means cannibal, although there is no evidence to show they did eat human flesh.

Villages were built in forest clearings, and each settlement had its own chieftain. Huts were round with timber walls and palm-thatched roofs. Early accounts from nearby islands show that they enjoyed dancing, either for pleasure or as part of rituals, and they played ball games. They were primarily fishermen and hunters, although they did cultivate kitchen gardens, and developed a system of shift cultivation, known as 'conuco'.

When the Caribs achieved dominance, they adopted or adapted many of the Arawak skills especially for farming and boat building, although their pottery was not as elaborate.

European arrival

The Portuguese explorer Pedro a Campos 'discovered' Barbados in 1536, and it is known that the Spanish visited the island in the early-16th century, probably looking for slave labor, and it is possible that they carried off all the Indians, or that if there were any survivors, they were wiped out by diseases introduced by the sailors.

Barbados was so small and so out of the way it was not worth their while settling the island, and by the mid-16th century, the Spanish virtually abandoned any claim to the island. The island probably gets its name from Portuguese sailors who visited in the late-16th century.

They thought the many hanging shoots from the branches of the strangler or 'bearded' figs, looked like beards, and so called the island Los Barbudos, meaning the bearded ones. Their word 'barba' for beard is also the origin of the English word barber. There is also a legend that the island was named after bearded Indians who inhabited it when the Portuguese arrived, but there is no evidence to support this.

The English arrived in Barbados in 1625 and like many of these early voyages of exploration, it was found more by luck than judgement. Captain John Powell aboard the *Olive* had no idea where he was when he landed on the deserted island. He was so impressed by it, however, that he formally laid claim to the island on behalf of the voyage's sponsor and returned to England with the news.

His patron Sir William Courteen ordered him back to the island to establish a colony, but on the way Powell captured a rich Spanish galleon and returned to England with his spoils. On hearing that the expedition had been abandoned, a furious Courteen immediately dispatched a second vessel, the *William and John*, which arrived at Holetown on 17 February 1627, and the first permanent settlement was established. Slavery also dates from that time, as the vessel brought ten African slaves who had been found aboard a Portuguese merchant ship captured during the voyage.

In 1627 the island was divided into 6 parishes, and in 1645 the boundaries were redrawn to provide for 11 parishes – Christ Church, St Andrew, St George, St James, St John, St Joseph, St Lucy, St Michael, St Peter, St Philip and St Thomas. For more than 320 years until 1969, the parishes collected local taxes and were responsible for maintaining churches and roads in their area and looking after the poor.

English settlement

The early years saw considerable feuding as the island was fought

(cont'd on page 16)

The Bajan Queen

Silver Rock

St James Beach Hotel, Tamarind Cove

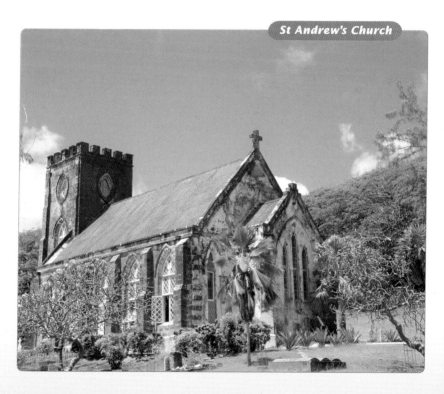

St Andrew's Church

over by the English aristocracy. The Earl of Carlisle laid claim to the island and sent out his own men to settle there, and by 1629 had wrested control from Courteen. During the 1630s the two sides continued to fight over control to such an extent that few crops were harvested and the settlement was near collapse. In 1639 a peace of a sort was brought about by the establishment of the House of Assembly by the Governor Henry Hawley. In effect, the parliament simply carried out the wishes of Hawley, but it did provide a forum for the two sides to air their grievances. The Barbados legislature is the second oldest in the Caribbean after Bermuda, and the third oldest in the Commonwealth.

The Assembly encouraged the immigration of more settlers and this further diluted the power of the Carlisle and Courteen camps.

The island's early development was hindered because of its geographic position and the strong prevailing winds. Sailing ships heading for Barbados generally had to approach from the east with the wind behind them, as trying to approach from the west was too dangerous because of the strong headwinds. However, once developed the location of Barbados became one of its strengths. It was the first landfall for ships travelling from Britain and mainland Europe to the eastern Caribbean and became an important port handling a three-way trade between Europe, the rest of the Caribbean and South America. Ships approaching from the east could be seen miles out at sea, and any vessels trying to approach from the west faced an imposing chain of forts. Because of this strategic position Barbados never faced serious attack and it was used as the headquarters of British naval forces in the eastern Caribbean.

The early years of English settlement continued to be traumatic. The island was not fought over by different nations as were most of the others in the Caribbean, but supply ships from England were often very late and the settlers had great difficulty in establishing suitable crops for export. Often when

A riotous royal night

By 1650 there were more than a hundred ale houses in Bridgetown, which was a preferred port of call for visiting seamen because everything they needed was provided in the town. It is said that the island's first hotel was built with the profits of a riotous evening enjoyed by the then Prince of Wales, Prince William Henry, who was enjoying shore leave with a number of his Royal Navy officer colleagues. Much of their partying was done in a house owned by Rachel Pringle, the most famous of the 'painted ladies' of the time. The house was almost wrecked but all the damage was added up and paid for in full by the Prince and his friends, and the money was used to build the island's first hotel.

they had a harvest there were not the ships available to transport it.

Economic growth

The first crops planted were tobacco and cotton but conditions were not ideal and competition was fierce. The tobacco did not match the quality of that grown in the Virginias, and cotton only produced profitable crops when grown near the coast.

In 1637 Dutchman Pieter Blower introduced sugar cane to the island, and in the 1640s with the help of Dutch planters from Brazil, there was a massive switch to sugar cane production which had an immediate impact on the island and was to shape its future for the next 300 years.

Island planters visited Brazil to bring back more cane, and to learn how it was processed to produce rum. A colony of Jews from Brazil also returned with the planters to Barbados and set up as merchants underwriting much of the massive expansion program. Their synagogue in Bridgetown is the oldest in the Western Hemisphere.

Barbados was the first island in the Caribbean to grow sugar cane and initially it was used only to produce rum. By the 1650s, however, the true worth of the crop was realized, but it was only profitable with a large, cheap work force and when grown on large acreages. The two immediate effects of the switch to sugar cane were the introduction of large numbers of slaves from Africa, and the amalgamation small estates into huge ones. A number of Arawak Indians were also brought to the island from Guyana to help teach the settlers how to cultivate tropical edible plants and fruits, and despite promises that they would be able to return home, they were also forced into slavery.

The impact of slavery

In the early 1640s, the island had a population of about 37,000 whites, mostly yeoman farmers and indentured servants, and some 6,000 Africans. Within 40 years, the number of whites had fallen to about 20,000 while the number of slaves had increased to around 46,000. And by 1690 there were about 15,000 whites and almost 60,000 slaves. When slavery was abolished in 1834 there were only 15,000 Europeans but more than 88,000 non-whites.

Although the number of land-owners decreased in the mid-1600s as estates became larger, large numbers of white people moved to Barbados. There were refugees from both sides in the Civil War and an agreement was reached on the island so that they could live without dispute. It was agreed that if a supporter of either side mentioned the words 'Royalist, Cavalier, Roundhead or Parliamentarian', they would have to provide a slap-up dinner for everyone within earshot at the time. The dinner was to consist of a suckling pig and turkey, and the agreement was locally referred to as the 'Turkey and Roast Pork Treaty'.

Presumably because the Parliamentarians were victorious in England, there were more Royalist emigrés to Barbados, and by the late 1640s they were in the majority. On 3 May 1650, they declared the island's loyalty to the Royalist cause, and in response the English Commonwealth Parliament dispatched a fleet to re-take the island. The Bermuda fleet arrived in October but rather than fight, the two sides sat down and agreed the Charter of Barbados, which was ratified by the English Parliament the following the year. Under the terms of the Charter, the Barbadians' right to freedom of religion was protected, there was to be no taxation without representation, a freeholder-elected Assembly and open ports were introduced.

In 1663 the English Crown, desperate for funds, introduced a unilateral tax on all exports from the island. Although this was clearly against the Charter, Charles II got round this by declaring that the island was now under his direct jurisdiction. The law was not repealed until 1838.

Other settlers arrived as indentured labor promising to work for five or seven years for just food and board but no wages in return for a grant of land at the end of their service. Few people realize that many Englishmen were actually deported to Barbados as virtual slaves. Many of the first shipments consisted of opponents to Oliver Cromwell, and the second wave came after the ill-fated Monmouth Rebellion in 1685 when the notorious Judge Jeffreys 'Barbadosed' many for their part in the uprising. It was also not uncommon for

drunks to be rounded up off the streets by gangs and carried aboard ship, only to sober up and discover they were bound for Barbados to work as indentured labor. Because of the island's remoteness, the major landowners had enormous powers and exercised them, especially over the slaves.

The slaves were so dominated that although there were sporadic minor incidents, most uprisings were swiftly and harshly suppressed. In many cases, informers tipped off the authorities who rounded up the ringleaders before trouble broke out. One such case was in 1675 when the authorities were tipped off shortly before the uprising was due to start. Six of the ringleaders were burnt alive and the rest were publicly beheaded. There was no serious slave uprising until the Bussa's Rebellion in 1816.

On the island, however, sugar was king, and massive fortunes were made. Sugar was so lucrative that every suitable piece of land was used for its cultivation because it was cheaper to import other foods. Sugar was often used instead of money, and when Willoughby Fort was built to defend Bridgetown and its harbor in 1656 its cost was billed as 80,000lbs of sugar.

In the late 17th century, Barbados had become known as the 'brightest jewel in the English crown'. The island's riches were also boosted by a flourishing smuggling industry. However, a smallpox epidemic at the end of the 17th century, killed thousands of planters, slaves and soldiers stationed on the island.

An old mill at Cove Bay

The eighteenth century

The Anglicizing of Barbados continued throughout the 18th century. Unlike many of the other islands where plantations were owned by rich absentee landlords in England, most of the land on Barbados was owned by families living on their estates. They built fabulous great houses and introduced a social order that still exists today. The first regular mailboat service between England and Barbados began in 1703, Codrington College, opened as a theological college in 1745, making it the oldest seminary in the Western Hemisphere. The island's first newspaper, the *Barbados Gazette* was established in 1731.

The prosperity of the first half of the 18th century contrasts with the crises of the second half. In 1760 most of the crop was lost because of attack by sugar ants. Bridgetown was almost completely destroyed by fire in 1776 and again the following year, and in 1780 the island was hit by a devastating hurricane which killed more than 4,000, flattened the crops and destroyed many of the island's buildings.

The nineteenth century

There was still enormous demand in Europe for sugar and it commanded high prices. Even when sugar beet was planted in Europe and sugar cane prices tumbled in the Caribbean, Barbados managed to survive largely because the newly freed slaves had nowhere else to go, and little alternative but

Freedom of the slaves

Although the British Parliament abolished slave trading in 1807, it did nothing to ease the plight of those already enslaved. In June 1815 a Bill was enacted in London to set up the Slave Registry Bill. Slaves on Barbados thought that this would lead to emancipation, and when they realized this was not the case, they planned an uprising to begin on Easter Sunday, 14 April 1816.

During the revolt, slaves burnt the cane fields and destroyed buildings and equipment, but it was harshly put down. Only one white died in the fighting but more than 170 slaves were killed, and afterwards, more than 200 slaves were executed and many others deported to plantations in Honduras.

The Emancipation Movement gained momentum in the 1820s with the Churches becoming increasingly outspoken against the inhumanity and injustice of slavery.

In 1834 the slaves were granted their 'freedom' under the Emancipation Act passed on 28 August, 1833, but there was a sting in the tail. Slaves were only to be freed after agreeing to complete a four year 'apprenticeship'. All slaves had to agree to stay with their masters for the next four years working for minimum wages, so it was not until 1 August, 1838 that there was true emancipation.

On most other Caribbean islands, under the apprentice-ship scheme slaves had to work free of charge for their old masters for three-quarters of the working work, but were given food and board and allowed to spend the rest of the time cultivating any land cleared from the forest. On Barbados, all the land was in the hands of the estate owners so there was no option of starting their own settlements. The freed slaves had to con-tinue working for their old masters or emigrate to seek new employment, and when the estate owners realized there was a labor drain they blocked emigration any way they could.

Emancipation Monument near Mangara

to carry on working for their former masters who owned all the land.

The landowners continued to flourish by paying near-slave wages and providing few basic services. An adult male slave was paid the equivalent of 35p (50c) a week, with a small bonus to cover the incredibly hard work cutting the harvest. In 1840 the Masters and Servants Act, effectively bound all former slaves as tenants to their old masters, and this led to the establishment of tenantries, known locally as chattel houses.

In 1854 a cholera epidemic swept the island and at least 20,000 people died. The general situation caused considerable social unrest and resulted in a number of protests, such as the 1876 Confederation Riots, all of which were harshly put down. In 1876 there were about 16,500 whites, 40,000 'colored' and 106,000 blacks, and the riots broke out because of a plan to scrap the island's leg-islative assembly and run Barbados as a Crown Colony. Governor John Pope-Hennessy had the job of im-plementing it and he stressed the benefits to the working classes.

The riots broke out, not because the islanders objected to the plan, but because the planters who held all the power, rejected it out of hand. The riots broke out on 20 April and lasted for 2 days. Mobs attacked scores of estates and did considerable damage but they were careful to avoid any loss of life, but in the fighting when the militia were called in, eight rioters were killed.

The Governor was transferred to Hong Kong, and in 1884 the

Sir Grantley Herbert Adams

number of people entitled to vote was increased slightly although the right to vote was still based on income and property ownership. William Conrad Reeves, of mixed parents, who was responsible for many significant changes for the good, including extending the franchise, was knighted and became Chief Justice in 1886, a position he held until 1902.

Into the twentieth century

In 1898 a hurricane destroyed thousands of homes, and in 1902 there was a major small-pox epidemic, followed by yellow fever in 1908. Falling sugar prices had a dramatic effect on the island. Up to 20,000 men left to find work on the Panama Canal project, and they sent money home, some of which was used to buy

Bridgetown

small plots of land from planters who were anxious to raise cash to keep their estates going. As sugar's profitability declined, many planters turned some acreages over to cotton and this was a successful crop until the First World War.

With battles waging across Europe production of sugar beet came almost to a standstill. With high demand for sugar, the cane producers were able to cash in but only until European production resumed after the war.

During the 1920s the price of sugar swung up and down, and this was a decade of major change. Income tax was introduced to help pay for public health, roads and agriculture, the Democratic League and Workingman's Association were founded, and the League's first candidate was elected to the House of Assembly.

While the new political parties espoused universal suffrage, free and compulsory education, and welfare benefits, it was not until the 1930s that there were serious political, economic and social changes. These were brought about because of the results of the Depression, a rising population and a virtual ban on emigration, an emerging middle class hungry for change and a growing sense of nationalism encouraged by people such as Jamaica's Marcus Garvey.

The social unrest led to strikes and riots, and in 1937 the West Indies Royal Commission, set up to look at social and economic conditions, recommended legal recognition of trade unions and extending the right to vote. These measures were introduced in the early 1940s and allowed the emerging black political parties to become dominant for the first time.

In 1944 women were given the vote, and universal suffrage was introduced in 1951. In 1954, the leader of the trade union movement, Grantley Adams became the island's first prime minister. In 1958 Barbados was a major influence in the establishment of the West Indies Federation, with the now Sir Grantley Adams elected its first leader. The Federation was dissolved in 1962, one year after Barbados has been granted full internal self-government.

The island remained in British possession until 30 November 1966. It was in English hands for so long and so moulded by English settlers, that it was known as 'Little England', the most British of all the Caribbean Islands.

Barbados achieved independence under the premiership of Errol Barrow. It is a member of the Commonwealth, was a founder member of the Caribbean Free Trade Area in 1968, which became Caricom in 1973. The two main political parties are the Democratic Labour Party (DLP) and the ruling Barbados Labour Party (BLP) led by Prime Minister Owen Arthur. The Governor General is Sir Clifford Husbands.

WEATHER

Barbados enjoys year-round good weather with an annual average temperature of around 80°F (27°C). The coolest months are January to April and the warmest July to September, and there are very few days when the sun makes no appearance.

Because of year round on-shore breezes, temperatures do not usually rise above 88°F (31°C) or fall below 70°F (24°C). The lowest temperature ever recorded is 59°F (15°C). The dry season lasts from mid-December to May and the wet season occupies the rest of the year, with August to October the wettest months. When it does rain, it can be torrential, but the downpours are usually short-lived and the sun is quickly out again. Downpours can also be remarkably localized with one area getting a soaking, and another, just a short distance away, remaining dry. Annual rainfall averages about 60 inches (152cm) a year and increases with altitude. Some coastal areas receive less than 40 inches (102cm) a year, while more than 95 inches (241cm) has been recorded in the mountains.

THE PEOPLE

Bajans are genuinely charming, generous and hospitable, and you should make time to get to know them. Barbadian society is traditionally a matriarchal one, with mothers and grandmothers looking after the children and often living apart from the father who visits. Couples living together usually do so without a formal wedding, so most children are born outside marriage and often referred to as 'outside children'. This tradition still exists today and stems directly from the slave system when the men and women were deliberately kept apart almost all of the time to prevent friendships and family ties developing.

Bridgetown is the capital and only port, and a third of the island's population live in or close to it. Most of the other islanders live either in the other towns of Oistins, Holetown and Speightstown, in villages, or 'tenantries' known locally as chattel houses.

Most of the farmland is owned by large estates and companies, and tenantries are groups of homes housing the workers. The workers own the homes but the land is owned by the estate, so there is no security of tenure. Because of its small size, Barbados is one of the most densely populated countries on earth, and there is little wasted space, but there are still

Hurricanes

Barbados lies in the hurricane belt and the hurricane season lasts from June to November, with August and the first half of September generally the most active months. The island has been badly hit many times over the last 300 years, but thankfully not for the last 40 years or so and before that in 1898. Most hurricanes originating off the west coast of Africa and sweeping across the Atlantic take a more northerly route, thankfully by-passing Barbados. Hurricane monitoring techniques are now very sophisticated and ample warning is given of any approaching tropical storm. If such a warning is given, act on advice given locally. There are clearly marked hurricane shelters throughout the island.

lots of areas to explore both inland and along the coastline.

About 92 per cent of the 263,500 population is of direct African or mixed descent and the rest come from Europe, North and South America, the East Indies or China. The 'High Whites' are the descendants of the island's old land owning ruling class, and typically characterized as more British than the British. While both their numbers and influence are declining, they have left an indelible mark on the island with institutions such as cricket, bridge clubs, polo and most of the place names.

'Redlegs'

The descendants of British indentured servants have long been called 'redlegs' because of the color of their skin after exposure to the sun. For many generations the redlegs were a distinct social group preferring to live and marry within their own communities, but for much of this century they have been marrying into, and absorbed by, the wider community.

Religion

Just under two thirds of the adult population regularly attend church, and the greater proportion of these are women. There are scores of different religious denominations represented on the island, the main ones being Anglican, Methodist, Moravian and Roman Catholic.

The Moravian Church was the first to send missionaries to the island with the specific task of bringing education to the slaves and converting them. They arrived in Barbados in 1765, more than twenty years before the Methodists who had the same aim. The Moravian Church started as a 15th century Protestant Reform movement, which emerged in Bohemia and Moravia many years before Luther. Despite ferocious attempts to suppress it, the church survived and established closed communities dedicated to contemplation and worship. In 1727, however, the church elders met and decided they had to move from being a closed order to becoming world-reach missionaries as the Church of the United Brethren.

Within five years missionaries had arrived in the West Indies where they set up missions and when allowed, schools to teach the slaves. On Barbados their first mission was at Sharon in St Thomas parish. The church was always outspoken in its support first for better treatment of the slaves, and then their freedom, and its congregation is still mostly black.

Other religious groups include the African Methodist Episcopal Church and the Tie Head Movement, which was started on Barbados by Granville Williams in 1957 when he established the Jerusalem Apostolic Spiritual Baptist Church at Ealing Grove. Followers wear turbans, which account for the group's name, and brightly colored robes – each of the colors has religious and spiritual significance. Services are wonderfully joyous events with unrestrained singing,

Rastafarians

Rastafarians are possibly the most misunderstood of all sects, partly perhaps because of the appearance of many of its adherents who, for religious reasons, wear their hair in dreadlocks, although this is not compulsory. Rastafarians are generally young, peace-loving, teetotal vegetarians, who worship the Black Messiah.

Their spiritual leader is the late Emperor Haile Selassie of Ethiopia, who they believe is still with them, and whose title includes 'ras' meaning prince and 'tafari' meaning 'to be feared'. They believe they are one of the lost tribes of Israel, descended directly from Solomon, and that Ethiopia is the Promised Land.

They do not smoke tobacco but many use 'sacred' ganja, which they smoke from a pipe called a chalice, which reinforces the religious symbolism attached to it. The red, black and green that Rastafarians wear, represent respectively, the blood of their martyrs, the color of their skin, and the green of the lush Caribbean vegetation which symbolizes hope.

Most prefer to commune with nature and avoid tourist areas, but there are Rasta imitators who may try to hustle for money, so be warned. A number of the island's artists, actors, musicians and sportsmen are Rastafarians.

handclapping and even dancing as the spirit moves the worshipers.

Many beliefs incorporate both Christian elements and African practices and folklore.

FOLKLORE

Folklore abounds on Barbados and many of the tales have been passed down by mouth from generation to generation. The stories were a means of preserving old myths and traditions, and incorporated African folklore, philosophy and moral tales.

However, many of the stories tell of duppies, malevolent spirits, roaming the countryside at night, and are full of symbolism about slavery, oppression and hardship. It is still common to find bunches of herbs hanging over doorways and windows to ward off **duppies**.

There are lots of other evil spirits, including heartmen who are said to prey on children.

Obeah, or African magic, still has a following and is a mixture of superstition and centuries-old tribal medicine suitably adapted to accommodate the herbs and plants of Barbados. There is no doubt that many of the herbal cures and potions do work. There are whispered tales of obeah curses and evil charms, and it is known that deeply held convictions and superstitions could induce great fear and sometimes death. Practising obeah is a criminal offence on the island and in the 1960s, a man accused of murdering his wife's lover had the charge reduced to manslaughter, when the court accepted that he was temporarily insane under the influence of obeah.

Perfect Combination – Sun, sea and sand

CULTURE

The cultural and artistic traditions of Barbados reflect the many races and nations that have been involved with the island's development over the last 2,000 years. The Arawak and Carib influence lives on in folklore, many food styles, traditional arts and crafts and place names such as Indian River. There is still a Spanish influence in the rhythms of the calypso, but the two strongest influences are of course, from African and English cultures, and while some have retained their individual identity, most have blended over the centuries especially in the areas of music, dance and the arts. The current cultural changes come from cable and satellite television, tourism and the large numbers of Bajans returning after visiting or living in Britain or the United States.

Music

Bajans, like all West Indians, love music and generally, the louder the better. There is traditional folk and drum music with its roots in West African rhythms, tuk with its roots in the early plantations, reggae and jazz, classical concerts and calypso. Calypso is Caribbean satire. The music is important but it is the words that count, and the more topical and hard hitting the better.

Many calypsos involve the audience who have to respond to questions posed by the singer, and it is thought this is how the music which originated in Africa, could have developed in the plantation fields – as both a means of uplifting spirits and secretly communicating with each other. Tony Carter, the Mighty Gabby, is regarded as the Bajan calypso King and every year there are several Calypso contests that attract talented songwriters and singers and aspiring pretenders to the crown. Soca is truly Barbadian and is even more upbeat than calypso with rhythms all of its own. Steel pan bands are a common feature providing foot-tapping music at tourist shows, while tuk bands have traditionally provided music for the Bajans.

Tuk bands

Because African drummers could express emotions and send messages by the way they drummed, the use of drums by slaves was banned in the late 17th century. Any drum found was destroyed, so the slaves improvised by drumming on logs. The name of the band comes from the 'tuk' noise made when the drumstick hits the log. As drums were permitted again, tuk bands emerged with large bass drums pounding out the pulsating beat, others giving the rhythm and a penny whistle providing the melody.

Theater

Theater thrives on Barbados whether as after dinner entertainment at hotels and resorts, or full blown drama in one of the island's theatres. **The Sherbourne Center** stages '*1627 And All That*', an evening presentation featuring the

The Barbados Heritage Passport

The passport is a very affordable way of discovering more about the country's rich history and culture. Organized by the Barbados National Trust, the passport allows holders to visit sixteen of its most impressive sites and historic buildings at substantially reduced cost. During the winter, the National Trust also organizes Great House tours. For more information contact the Barbados National Trust, Ronald Tree House, 10th Avenue, Belleville, St Michael (☎ 426-2421).

Barbados Dance Theater twice a week – Sunday and Thursday in a light hearted look at the island's history. There are productions at the **Queen's Park Theatre** and **The Auditorium**, and drama features prominently during the annual **Crop Over Festival** both at the National Stadium and Farley Hill Park.

The **Barbados Dance Theater Company**, founded by Mary Stevens in 1968, is a wonderfully vibrant ensemble, which blends modern dance and traditional African. The **Rontana Dance Movement** specializes in dance choreographed to the beat and rhythm of the drum, and there are a number of other fine dance troupes specializing in everything from classical ballet and jazz, to folk and experimental.

Writers, art & crafts

Barbados has also produced a wealth of artistic talent, and since the 1950s this has been boosted by the **Barbados National Arts Council**. There are fine writers such as **George Lamming**, and poets, and artistic talent can also be seen in the form of murals on the walls of shops in Bridgetown's Baxter Road and road side vendor's carts, sculptures and paintings adorning public buildings and the island's many galleries, including the **Barbados Arts Council Gallery** in the Pelican Village (☎ 426-4385), the **Queen's Park Gallery** (☎ 427-2345), and the **Coffee and Cream Art Gallery** in Paradise Village, St Lawrence Gap (☎ 428-2708), which features a large number of the island's up and coming talent. Also worth visiting are the **Verandah Art Gallery**, Broad Street, Bridgetown, which features original local art, pottery and prints, and **Artwork** at the Quayside Centre, Rockley (☎ 435-8112) which features Bajan and Caribbean arts and crafts.

There are many others such as the **Studio Art Gallery**, Fairchild Street, Bridgetown (☎ 427-5463), **Talma Mill Art Gallery**, Christ Church, by appointment (☎ 428-9383), **Earthworks Pottery and Gallery**, Edgehill Heights (☎ 425-0223), **Dayrell's Gallery**, St George, by appointment (☎ 437-9400), **Fine Art Framing**, St Michael's Row, Bridgetown (☎ 426-5325) and the family-run **Fairfield Pottery and Gallery**, Fairfield Cross Road (☎ 424-3800) which is the largest pottery on the island.

There are also many opportunities to visit the studios of artists such as **Gail Hermicks,** at Cliff Plantation, **Omowali Stewart** at Clermont Gardens, and **Ras Ishi Butcher** at Sealy Hall. There are also woodcarvers, paper makers, potters, weavers and batik designers throughout the island.

Craftsmen of particular note include **James Alfred Massiah,** a master craftsman, whose coral carvings and sculptures adorn many of the island's great houses. **Karl Broodhagen** is the sculptor responsible for the 'Bussa' Emancipation statue near the Sherbourne Centre on highway 5.

The making and flying of kites is an art form, and there is a major kite competition on Easter Sunday at Garrison Savannah.

The Crop Over Festival

The festival was traditionally held to celebrate the gathering in of the sugar cane harvest. Now revived it's the excuse for a major two-week long summer party, a combination of Caribbean Thanksgiving, Harvest Festival and Bajan Carnival. The celebration starts in mid-July and runs through into August. The traditional celebration after the incredibly grueling task of harvesting the sugar cane was one of the few occasions the slaves had during the year to enjoy themselves, and the Crop Over Festival reflects this.

The Ceremonial Delivery of the Last Canes is the link between the modern Crop Over Festival and the old one, and it includes a toast to the workers of the sugar industry and the crowning of the King and Queen of the Crop – the champion cutters.

There are decorated cart and costume parades, band and calypso competitions, gourmet events as part of the Bridgetown Market, and the Cohobblopot, an extraordinary mix of music and drama at the National Stadium during which the King and Queen of Bands are crowned. The Calypso King is named after the aptly named Pic-o-de-Crop contest, and there are several calypso tents in which you can listen to the artists.

The highlight of the festival is **Kadooment Day**, on the first Monday of August, when the island's bands and Bajans take to the streets in their highly ornate and imaginative costumes for the final parade before a spectacular night-time firework display. There is also the Kiddies Kadooment, when the children dress up and parade. This is not a time for those who like peace and quiet, as pulsating music booms out from dawn until late at night (although it is still possible to find festival-free parts of the island). It is a great occasion, however, and a thoroughly enjoyable one and you should get in there and 'jam' with the best of them.

Although the main Crop Over Festival events are held in Bridgetown, the whole island takes part and there are 'jump-ups' and fetes in villages throughout Barbados.

FESTIVALS

The **Holetown Festival** is held every February and commemorates the arrival of the first English settlers in 1627. The week long festival has a near Carnival atmosphere with lots of music, dancing and singing, band concerts and church services. The **St James Parish Church** is always worth visiting during the festival because of its magnificent flower arrangements. The main event is a massive Street Fair.

The **Oistins Fish Festival** takes place around Easter and is a celebration of the island's fishermen and the fishing industry, and in recent years, the arts as well. Events range from fishing competitions and boat racing to crab racing, and there is lots of music, an arts and crafts display and plenty of delicious food stalls. Easter is an important time both religiously and socially, and you will see wonderful Easter bonnets being worn on Easter Day.

The **National Independence Festival of Creative Arts** (NIFCA) is held in November, is a celebration of the creative arts with shows and competitions for dancing, singing, music, drama, crafts and writing. The winners are announced on Independence Day 30 November.

GOVERNMENT

Barbados has a British-style government with the Queen as head of state, and represented on the island by the Governor-General.

Prime Minister's office, Bridgetown

There is an elected **House of Assembly** and an appointed **Senate**. All islanders over the age of eighteen can vote. Elections for the House of Assembly are held every five years.

ECONOMY

Agriculture, offshore finance, light manufacturing and tourism are the main industries. There are some deposits of oil and natural gas. Most of the land is suitable for agriculture and as sugar cane acreages have declined because of lower world demand and falling prices, more vegetables and fruit have been grown and more land turned over for fodder and livestock production with cattle, sheep, pigs and goats. There is also some cotton.

Most of the cane is grown on large estates, and there are also about 30,000 farmers with holdings of half an acre (0.2 hectares) or less, producing yams, beans, sweet potato, okra, taro, beet, cabbage, pumpkin, squash, peppers and salad plants.

Flowers are grown commercially for export and fishing is a major industry although mostly for home consumption.

There is some quarrying for clay, limestone and sand, and imported crude oil is refined for local needs. There has been a considerable growth in manufacturing industries which include food processing, cement, cigarette manufacturing, paper products, rum, chemicals, machinery, fuel, electrical components and clothing. Tourism is the largest foreign exchange earner, with more than 1 million visitors every year, half of them from cruise ships.

NATURAL HISTORY

Flora

Despite its small size, the island has a variety of habitats because of different vegetation zones, and centuries of planting by immigrants.

Originally the island was covered entirely by trees which were rapidly cleared for plantations and the timber used for building or shipped overseas. In little more

Mangroves

White mangroves can be found in many places around the island and if you look carefully at the leaves, you can usually see grains of salt, which are secreted by the plant. Red mangroves are much rarer on the island and generally only found in the **Graeme Hall Swamp**. Mangroves produce seedlings but not seeds. The arrow-like seedlings actually start growing while still attached to the parent tree, and when conditions are ripe they drop off, either embedding themselves into the mud below, or drifting away to take root elsewhere. Because mangroves usually grow in unstable muddy water, they produce prolific root systems above and below ground. Old trees generally have very impressive buttress roots above ground or at water level, as well as support roots which drop down from higher boughs.

than 100 years, because of the demand for ever more land for sugar cane plantations, more than three-quarters of all the forests have been cleared. Ironically timber was used to heat the huge cauldrons in which the sugar cane was boiled to produce molasses, then timber and coal from England had to be imported to fuel the industry.

Because Barbados is so small in area rain clouds from the east often pass over without dropping any precipitation, which then falls on the Windward Islands of St Lucia and St Vincent. Because of the lower rainfall, the vegetation, while still lush, is not as prolific as on the neighboring islands to the west.

There are distinct vegetation zones, although agricultural land, and mostly sugar cane fields, dominates. The main vegetation zones consist of lush, tropical coastline with coconut palms and mangrove swamps, small areas of original forest and tropical rain forest. This consisits of: mahogany, originally introduced from Honduras; lignum vitae; fustic; West Indian cedar; giant vines; huge stands of towering bamboo; and plantations and gardens. Cacti grow in the drier areas.

The mahogany, with its beautiful red and black seeds, was imported from Honduras towards the end of the 18th century and many of the other species now found throughout the island are not natives.

Another import is the towering casuarina, which originally came from Australia, thus its alternative name of Australian pine. It is thought to have been planted in Barbados in the mid-19th century as a wind break.

The tamarind tree

The tamarind, which is a native of the Far East, is thought to have been introduced in the mid-17th century via Central America. It is said that the tough branches of the tamarind were cut and used as canes to flog the slaves. The trees grow very old and to a height of 150 feet (46m), which is why many islanders call it the 'mile tree'. They produce pods containing a pulp which has a number of culinary uses – it is used to make a refreshing drink, and tamarind when dried is used as a spice in curries and preserves. The pods are also sent to England where the reddish-black pulp is an ingredient in the piquant famous Worcestershire Sauce. When too overripe to eat, the pulp can be used to polish metals, especially copper and brass.

If you spot a tamarind tree look at the ground around the trunk which is usually clear of any other vegetation. This is because the roots give off a toxic chemical which kills competing vegetation, a remarkable piece of evolutionary self-preservation. One reason tamarinds grow to such a grand old age is that they are very tough and with their deep root system they are able to withstand long periods of drought.

Century plants at Bathsheba

Above: Palms at Andromeda Gardens
Below: Mangrove

Above: Bougainvillea
Right: Hibiscus

34

Scotland District & Clark Hill

There are many wonderful ornamental gardens and most homes take great pride in cultivating wonderful floral displays.

The **Barbados Horticultural Society** was established in 1927 and is affiliated to the British Royal Horticultural Society. It promotes horticulture of all types, arranges exhibitions and open gardens. The society's annual flower show is held in February, and is open to both amateur and commercial gardeners, and the displays are always stunning.

There are tracts of rolling green land which reflect their former owners and look as if they might be parts of the English countryside – except for the palm trees. There are wonderful flowering plants and trees such as jasmine, orchids, hibiscus, poinsettia, thryallis and bougainvillea, and the spreading cotton tree, which can grow to be hundreds of years old. Although hibiscus and bougainvillea bloom everywhere, neither is native to the islands. Bougainvillea, named after a French explorer, was brought to the West Indies from Brazil in the early 1700s, while the hibiscus comes from Hawaii.

The flamboyant (poinciana) tree with its spectacular red flowers originally came from Madagascar, while the tulip tree, which bursts into a canopy of red blossom, comes from West Africa. The frangipani, which was introduced at the beginning of the 18th century, is one of the island's most spectacular flowering trees. The wild frangipani is also known as the jasmine tree because of its heavily-scented blossom and always has white flowers, while its cultivated cousin, the red frangipani has spectacular pink, red or orange flowers. There is also a yellow-blossomed frangipani.

The national flower is the **Pride of Barbados**, although it is not known if it is a native of the island, or an early import from Central America. It is often grown as an ornamental garden flower, thus one of its other names of 'flower fence'. It also grows widely in the wild.

There are many species of palm, especially the royal or cabbage palm, which grows alongside many of the island's roads. It is called the cabbage palm because the young bud resembles a cabbage, and it is eaten as a vegetable. The traveler's palm is also common with its wedge of fan-shaped leaves. It gets its name because the leaves were said to grow on an east to west axis, but this is not true, so do not rely on this for navigating.

The century plant is also common and blooms only once in its life. It flowers after about ten years with a fantastic spread of blooms, and then the plant dies as its seeds are scattered.

Other common tree species include West Indian cedar, Spanish elm, boxwood, red-barked turpentine, bearded fig, strangler fig, bay rum, sandbox, satinwood, rosewood, fiddlewood, kapok, yellow cedar, mahoe, wattle, cinnamon and buttonwood. In many gardens you can see the shack-shack, a species of ebony also known as mother-in-law's tongue. Long pods dangle from the branches and clatter against each other in the wind. The wood produces a wonderful finish and is used by sculptors, woodcarvers and furniture makers.

The silk cotton tree, or devil's tree, is held in awe because according to folklore the trees are the souls of dead slaves. Its Latin name is *ceiba pentandra*, and it is thought

Warning – the manchineel

The manchineel, which can be found on many beaches, has a number of effective defensive mechanisms which can prove very painful. Trees vary from a few feet to more than 30 feet (9 m) in height, and have widely spreading, deep forked boughs with small, dark green leaves and yellow stems, and fruit like small, green apples. If you examine the leaves carefully without touching them, you will notice a small pinhead sized raised dot at the junction of leaf and leaf stalk. The apple-like fruit is poisonous, and sap from the tree causes very painful blisters, and was used as a poison.

It is so toxic, that early Caribs are said to have dipped their arrow heads in it before hunting trips, and an effective, and apparently often used untraceable method of killing someone in olden times, was to add a few drops of the sap to their food over a period.

The sap is released if a leaf or branch is broken, and more so after rain. Avoid contact with the tree, don't sit under it, or on a fallen branch, and do not eat the fruit. If you do get sap on your skin, run into the sea and wash it off as quickly as possible.

that the *ceiba* comes from an old word for canoe, as the tree was traditionally used by Amerindians to make dugout canoes. The tree produces fine kapok – silk cotton – used for stuffing, and its flowers, which open after sunset, attract bats.

The bay tree is from the Windward Islands, a member of the Laurel family and can grow to a height of 30 feet (9m). The leaves can be crushed for their oil which is used in the perfume industry. The leaves are used in cooking.

Many of the trees are grown for their fruit. These include the fig, mango, genip, chilli plum, cherry, almond, guava, golden and sugar apple, pomegranate, sapodilla, star apple, soursop, coconut, tamarind and breadfruit. The seagrape, which can be found along many beaches, produces edible fruit, but is much more important because its roots prevent sand erosion.

There are many species of orchid, mostly in the hills, and hundreds of different species of ferns and grasses.

Marine life

The marine environment is spectacular. There are scores of species of brightly-colored fish to be seen in and around the coral reefs. There are angelfish, doctor fish, sergeant fish, marine jewels and cavalla. The warm waters teem with larger fish, especially game fish such as tarpon, yellow-fin tuna, barracuda, jacks, sailfish, marlin, mackerel, sawfish, swordfish, snapper and kingfish or wahoo. There are also several species of sharks to be found in the offshore waters, as well as flying fish, served spicy as the national dish. You can see them being landed at the Carenage during the season, and then dine on them later.

There are also Queen conch, southern stingray, long-spined black sea urchin, and you have to be on the look out for Portuguese Man of War, whose tentacles can give a nasty sting.

Coral

Coral is very delicate and should not be touched and never damaged or removed. Some coral, such as fire coral, needs treating with great caution, but most are beautifully colored and safe, and are meant to be enjoyed. There are more than fifty species of coral, and the most common include seafan, staghorn, elkhorn, gorgonian, brain, large star, pillar, rose and orange reef.

Coral reefs are the ocean's equivalent to tropical rain forests, and only grow in waters with a year-round temperature above 68°F (20°C). Stony coral grows less than a half an inch (1.25cm) a year, and staghorn, the fastest growing coral in the Caribbean, only grows between 4 and 6 inches (10 to 15cm) a year. There are hundreds of types of shells and the inshore waters and beaches are a shell collector's dream.

Rockley Beach

Animals

Wildlife on Barbados has been a victim of intensive agriculture over the centuries and the resulting loss of habitat. Many species have become extinct including the Bajan parrot, which was finally wiped out by hunting and the monkeys which ate the eggs and young nestlings. Almost all the large animals today are farm livestock or domestic pets.

However, island wildlife does include many species of bats and butterflies. There is also the black-faced, small Barbados green monkey brought across on the slave ships from West Africa more than 300 years ago. It is not a large monkey which is probably why it has survived so well, although it is regarded as a pest and islanders collect a reward for every 'tail' turned in. You can still see it swinging through the trees, or darting across the road, so it is not too unusual to witness an occasional victim of a road accident.

Other animals include the hare and mongoose, and both are considered pests by farmers. The mongoose was introduced from Jamaica – to kill rats and poisonous snakes which thrived in the sugar cane fields. It killed all the snakes and has been known to attack young lambs, as well as taking other wild animals, eggs and fledgelings. You will probably see them rushing across the road.

Insects

The island has the usual array of insects with flies, grasshoppers, butterflies, moths, bees, ants and centipedes. Mosquitoes can be a problem especially in late afternoon, and sandflies are a pest. Known locally as merrywings, they prefer sand that is above the high tide line.

Birdlife

There is a varied birdlife with a number of native species. There are two species of hummingbird, dove, tanager, kingbird, egret, yellow breast, cowbird, parakeet, finch, thrush, warbler, grackle, plover, crows, and birds of prey. The two species of hummingbird are the curve-billed emerald-throat hummer, and the smaller straight-billed Antillean crested hummer, also known as the doctor bird. The male doctor bird has blue-green crest and despite its tiny size, ferociously defends its territory.

The sugar bird, or yellow-breasted bananaquit, is probably the yellow bird featured in the famous calypso of the same name, and is easily recognized by the vivid red patch on its bill.

Winter visitors include the colorful Christmas bird, wood sandpipers from North America, ruff, Greenland wheatear and black-headed gulls.

Around the coast you might see brown pelicans performing their aerial acrobatics before plunging into the sea after fish. There are also terns, sandpipers and the long-winged majestic black frigate birds.

Fruits

Bananas

Bananas are one of the Caribbean's most important exports, thus their nickname 'green gold' – and they grow everywhere.

There are three types of banana plant; the bananas that we normally buy in supermarkets originated in Malaya and were introduced into the Caribbean in the early 16th century by the Spanish. The large bananas, or plantains, originally came from southern India, and are largely used in cooking. They are often fried and served as an accompaniment to fish and meat. The third variety is the red banana, which is not grown commercially, but which can occasionally be seen around the island. A banana produces a crop about every nine months, and each cluster of flowers grows into a hand of bananas. A bunch can contain up to twenty hands of bananas, with each hand having up to 20 individual fruit.

Although they grow tall, bananas are not trees but herbacious plants which die back each year. Once the plant has produced fruit, a shoot from the ground is cultivated to take its place, and the old plant dies. Bananas need a lot of attention, and island farmers will tell you that there are not enough hours in a day to do everything that needs to be done. The crop needs fertilizing regularly, leaves need cutting back, and you will often see the fruit inside blue tinted plastic containers, which protect it from insect and bird attack, and speed up maturation.

Breadfruit

Breadfruit was introduced to the Caribbean by Captain Bligh in 1793. He brought 1,200 breadfruit saplings from Tahiti aboard the *Providence*, and these were first planted in Jamaica and St Vincent

Breadfruit & the mutiny on the *Bounty*

It was Bligh's attempts to bring in young breadfruit trees that led to the mutiny on the *Bounty* four years earlier. Bligh was given the command of the 215-ton *Bounty* in 1787 and was ordered to take the breadfruit trees from Tahiti to the West Indies where they were to be used to provide cheap food for the slaves.

The ship had collected its cargo and had reached Tonga when the crew, under Fletcher Christian, mutinied. The crew claimed that Bligh's regime was too tyrannical, and he and eighteen members of the crew who stayed loyal to him, were cast adrift in an open boat. The cargo of breadfruit was dumped overboard. Bligh, in a remarkable feat of seamanship, navigated the boat for 3,600 miles (5796km) until making landfall on Timor in the East Indies.

Some authorities have claimed that it was the breadfruit tree cargo that sparked the mutiny, as each morning the hundreds of trees in their heavy containers had to be carried on deck, and then carried down into the hold at nightfall. It might have proved just too much for the already overworked crew.

and then quickly spread throughout the islands.

Whatever the reason for the mutiny on the *Bounty*, breadfruit is a cheap carbohydrate-rich food, although pretty tasteless when boiled. It is best eaten fried, baked or roasted over charcoal. The slaves did not like it at first, but the trees spread and can now be found almost everywhere. It has large dark, green leaves and the large green fruits can weigh 10-12lbs (4.5-5.4kg). The falling fruits explode with a loud bang and splatter the pulpy contents over a large distance. It is said that no one goes hungry when the breadfruit is in season.

Calabash

The trees are native to the Caribbean and have huge gourd-like fruits which are very versatile when dried and cleaned. They can be used as water containers and bowls, bailers for boats, and as lanterns. Juice from the pulp is boiled into a concentrated syrup and used to treat coughs and colds, and the fruit is said to have many other medicinal uses.

Cinnamon

Also related to the laurel, cinnamon comes from the bark of an evergreen tree. The bark is rolled into 'sticks' and dried, and then ground or sold in small pieces. It is used as a spice, for flavoring, and adds a sweet, aromatic flavor to many dishes. Oil from the bark is used to flavor sweets, soaps, toothpastes and liqueurs, while oil from the leaves is used in perfumes. It is usually imported from the 'Spice Island of Grenada'.

Cocoa

Another important crop but is now largely imported from Grenada. Its Latin name *theobroma* means 'food of the gods'. A cocoa tree can produce several thousand flowers a year, but only a tiny fraction of these will develop into seed bearing pods. It is the heavy orange pods that hang from the cocoa tree which contain the beans which contain the seeds that produce cocoa and chocolate. The beans, containing a sweet, white sap that protects the seeds, are split open and kept in trays to ferment.

This process takes up to eight days and the seeds must be kept at a regular temperature to ensure the right flavor and aroma develops and then the seeds are dried.

In the old days people used to walk barefoot over the beans to polish them to enhance their appearance. Today, the beans are crushed to extract cocoa butter, and the remaining powder is cocoa. Real chocolate is produced by mixing cocoa powder, cocoa butter and sugar.

You can sometimes buy cocoa balls in the markets and village shops, which make a delicious drink. Each ball is the size of a large cherry. Simply dissolve the ball in a pan of boiling water, allow to simmer and then add sugar and milk or cream, for a rich chocolate drink. Each ball will make about four mugs of chocolate.

Grapefruit

Grapefruit is claimed as a Barbadian creation. A large citrus fruit known as a shaddock was introduced to

Enjoy romantic sunsets all year round

Coconut

Coconut palms are everywhere and should be treated with caution. Anyone who has heard the whoosh of a descending coconut and leapt to safety, knows how scary the sound is. Those who did not hear the whoosh, presumably did not live to tell the tale. Actually, very few people do get injured by falling coconuts and that is a near miracle in view of the tens of thousands of palms all over the island, but it is not a good idea to picnic in a coconut grove!

Coconut trees are incredibly hardy, able to grow in sand and even when regularly washed by salty seawater. They can also survive long periods without rain. Their huge leaves, up to 20 feet (6m) long in mature trees, drop down during dry spells so a smaller surface area is exposed to the sun which reduces evaporation. Coconut palms can grow up to 80 feet (29m) tall, and produce up to 100 seeds a year. The seeds are the second largest in the plant kingdom, and these fall when ripe.

The coconut traditionally bought in greengrocers back home, is the seed with its layer of coconut surrounded by a hard shell. This shell is then surrounded by a layer of copra, a fibrous material, and this is covered by a large green husk. The seed and protective coverings can weigh 30lbs (13.5kg) and more. The seed and casing is waterproof, drought proof and able to float, and this explains why coconut palms which originated in the Pacific and Indian Oceans, are now found throughout the Caribbean – the seeds literally floated across the seas.

The coconut palm is extremely versatile. The leaves can be used as thatch for roofing, or cut into strips and woven into hats, mats and baskets, while the husks yield coir, a fiber resistant to salt water and ideal for ropes and brushes and brooms. Green coconuts contain a delicious thirst-quenching 'milk', and the coconut 'meat' can be eaten raw, or baked in ovens for two days before being sent to processing plants where the oil is extracted. Coconut oil is used in cooking, soaps, synthetic rubber and even in hydraulic brake fluid.

As you drive around the island, you might see groups of men and women splitting the coconuts in half with machetes preparing them for the ovens.

the West Indies from Polynesia in the 18th century although why is not clear, as it had a thick skin, lots of seeds, almost no juice and a sour taste. A planter crossed the shaddock with an orange, and the result was the grapefruit. If you have never eaten a grapefruit fresh from the tree, take the opportunity to do so, as you will be amazed at how sweet and juicy it is. When freshly picked the peel can easily be removed, but after a few days the skin starts to contract round the fruit and it is this that imparts extra bitterness.

Guava

Common throughout the island, the aromatic, pulpy fruit is also a favorite with birds who then distribute its seeds. The fruit-bearing shrub can be seen on roadsides and in gardens, and it is used to make a wide range of products from jelly to 'cheese', a paste made by mixing the fruit with sugar. The fruit which ranges from a golf ball to a tennis ball in size, is a rich source of vitamin A and contains lots more vitamin C than citrus fruit.

Mango

Mango can be delicious if somewhat messy to eat. It originally came from India but is now grown throughout the Caribbean and found wherever there are people. Young mangoes can be stringy and unappetizing, but ripe fruit from mature trees which grow up to 50 feet (18m) and more, are usually delicious, and can be eaten raw or cooked. The juice is a great reviver in the morning, and the fruit is often used to make jams and other preserves. The wood of the mango is often used by boat builders.

Nutmeg

The trees originally came from the Banda Islands in Indonesia and for centuries its source was kept secret because it was such a valuable commodity to the merchants selling it. In 1770 a French naturalist raided the islands, then under Dutch control, and stole several hundred plants and seedlings which were planted on Mauritius and in French Guyana, but these almost all died.

At the end of the 18th century Britain was at war with Napoleon Bonaparte and Holland, which had allied with France. The British captured the Banda Islands during the war and before they handed them back in 1802, as part of the Treaty of Amiens, they had learnt the secret of the nutmeg and successfully planted it in Penang in Malaya and tropical territories around the world, including the West Indies.

The tree thrives in hilly, wet areas and the fruit is the size of a small tomato. The outer husk, or pericarp, which splits open while still on the tree, is used to make the very popular nutmeg jelly, delicious when spread on toast, desserts or meat. Inside, the seed is protected by a bright red casing which when dried and crushed, produces the spice mace. Finally, the dark outer shell of the seed is broken open to reveal the nutmeg that is dried and then ground into a powder, or sold whole so that it can be grated to add flavor to dishes.

In Victorian times it was fashionable to carry a nutmeg or wear it in a pendant to ward off illness, and the islanders still use grated nutmeg to help fight colds. Nutmeg trees are found on Barbados but Grenada together with Indonesia are the world's largest producers.

Passion fruit

The fruit is not widely grown but it can sometimes be bought at the market. The pulpy passion fruit contains hundreds of tiny seeds, and many people prefer to press the fruit and drink the juice. It is also commonly used in fruit salads, sherbets and ice creams.

Pawpaw

Pawpaw trees are also found throughout the Caribbean islands and are commonly grown in gardens. The trees are prolific fruit producers, but grow so quickly that the fruit soon becomes difficult to gather. The large, juicy melon-like fruits are eaten fresh, pulped for juice or used locally to make jams, preserves and ice cream.

They are rich sources of vitamin A and C. The leaves and fruit contain an enzyme which tenderizes meat, and tough joints cooked wrapped in pawpaw leaves or covered in slices of fruit, usually taste like much more expensive cuts. The same enzyme, papain, is also used in chewing gum, cosmetics, the tanning industry and, somehow, in making wool shrink-resistant. A tea made from unripe fruit is said to be good for lowering high blood pressure.

Pigeon peas

The plants are widely cultivated and can be found in many back gardens, they are also very hardy and drought resistant and give prolific yields of peas which can be eaten fresh or dried and used in soups and stews.

Pineapples

Pineapples were certainly grown in the Caribbean by the time Columbus arrived, and were probably brought from South America by the Amerindians. The fruit is slightly smaller than the Pacific pineapple, but the taste more intense.

Sugar apple & soursop

A member of the annona fruit family, it grows wild and in gardens throughout the islands. The small, soft sugar apple fruit can be peeled off in strips when ripe, and

Bougainvillea Beach Resort

Sugar Cane

S ugar cane is still the major commercial crop on the island. The canes can grow up to 12 feet (3.5 m) tall and after cutting, have to be crushed to extract the sugary juice. A good harvest produces about 30 tons an acre, and it takes between 8 and 9 tons of cane to produce one ton of sugar. Production has steadily declined over the past 10 years. Most estates had their own sugar mill powered by water wheels or windmills. The remains of many of these mills can still be seen around the island, as well as much of the original machinery, mostly made in Britain. After extraction, the juice is boiled until the sugar crystallizes. The mixture remaining is molasses and this is either exported, largely to the US and UK, or used to produce rum.

is like eating thick apple sauce. It can be eaten fresh or used to make sherbet or drinks. Soursop, is a member of the same family, and its spiny fruits can be seen in hedgerows and gardens. It is eaten fresh or used for preserves, drinks and ice cream.

Turmeric

Turmeric comes from the dried root and underground stems of a plant, which is a relative of ginger. The bright yellow spice is used to flavor foods, and as a coloring, in English mustard for instance. It is also used as a dye, and mostly imported from Grenada.

Vanilla

The vanilla plant is a climbing member of the orchid family which produces long, dangling pods containing beans. The vanilla is extracted by distilling the beans and is used as a food flavoring, and mostly imported from Grenada.

FOOD

You can dine in style enjoying international cuisines from around the world, or the best of Bajan Creole cooking. You can experiment with local tropical vegetables and enjoy the freshest of fish and shellfish, or sample the many ethnic restaurants, from Mexican to Chinese and Lebanese to finest French.

There are fast food outlets, both US and Bajan-style, for those who want to eat in a hurry and get back out into the sun as quickly as possible. Remember, however, that this is still the Caribbean and there is not the same degree of urgency experienced elsewhere, so if you think things are taking a long time, order another drink, relax and take in the view.

One of the great attractions is being able to dine alfresco. Most hotel and large restaurants accept credit cards but to avoid embarrassment always check first to make sure that if you do need cash you have enough. Dining out is not only fun but also very affordable.

It seems a shame to visit Barbados and not enjoy the excellent local spicy dishes, especially in true Bajan eateries, which offer excellent value.

Snacks

Eating on the move or out of doors can be very enjoyable, and there are many opportunities to eat from the snack bars on the street or by the beach. This 'street food' ranges from juices and ice creams flavored with local fruits, to hot snacks such as fritters, roasted corn, pork chops, patties and pates, which are pastry envelopes filled with seafood or spiced meat, especially beef, and rotis. Rotis originated in the East Indies and are another form of soft pastry envelope (chapati) stuffed with curried meats or vegetables. Take care if ordering a chicken roti, because in many places the meat contains small bones, which some people like to chew on! Most of this food is fried but it is usually wholesome, delicious and cheap. Bajan 'fast food' is traditionally served with rice and sweet potatoes, yams or beans.

Fish

There is wonderfully fresh seafood, especially lobster, yellow fin tuna, grouper and wahoo, a large mackerel type fish. Island specialties include salted codfish and codballs which are delicious. Flaked salted fish is mixed with eggs, milk, butter and seasoning and deep fried in boiling lard, the reason why they are so tasty. The codballs or fishcakes are often sold in rum

Bajan food

The great attraction of Bajan cooking is that it is a blend of so many other cuisines. Some cooking styles and flavors have been passed down from the Arawak Indians, others were introduced from Africa, India and China, there are still traces of Spanish, and you can still be offered traditional English dishes. The over riding emphasis in all Bajan food, however, is fresh, natural and spicy, with food purchased, prepared and served as quickly as possible.

shops and eaten inside a roll or bun. Another specialty is the roe of sea urchins served with chopped onions and sweet peppers and steamed or fried.

The Barbados national dish is flying fish and cou cou that can be served in a variety of ways. The fish are caught between December and June and served fresh during the season, with enough frozen to maintain supplies during the rest of the year. Restaurants and cooks all boast their own special flying fish seasoning is the best. It is traditionally made from black and red pepper, paprika, onion, garlic, parsley and thyme and seasonings, and other 'secret' herbs and spices. The fish is coated with the seasoning and then steamed, baked or pan fried, and served with a twist of lime. It is so popular there is even a shop at the airport selling vacuum-sealed, frozen flying fish fillets.

Tradtional dishes

Dishes that can be traced back to African cuisines include cou cou (or kush kush) which is made from cornmeal and okra and traditionally served with saltfish. It is the island equivalent of mashed potato and used to be a staple food of the slaves because it was so cheap, but it is now more spicy and makes a great meal.

Jug-jug is Bajan haggis, and made by blending guinea corn, green peas, salt pork and beef, fat, herbs and spices. It is said that Scots exiled to Barbados after the Monmouth Rebellion in 1685 could not find the traditional ingredients for haggis – oatmeal, minced liver, suet and blood – so improvised with what was available. The result was jug-jug and it is still traditionally served at Christmas in many districts.

Try Caribbean black bean, yellow bean and pumpkin or red pea soup, pumpkin soup, conch chowder or calalu (callaloo), a rich soup made from the huge leaves of the dasheen plant, also called elephant ears, and okra with flakes of fish, crab and meat and grated coconut, and spiced up with pepper. Pepperpot soup can be another meal in itself, made with salted meat and vegetables with local spices and seasonings.

The pepper pot is a staple Caribbean utensil. On Barbados it is sometimes called a cohobblepot, because it stands on the hob by the fire. The pepper pot is one of the innovations brought to the Caribbean by the Caribs. They discovered that the pulped root of the cassava tree produced a liquid called casareep, which was a preservative. Meat boiled in the liquid could be kept edible for indefinite periods, and this practice is the basis today of the famous Bajan

Special treats

These include cutters which are French bread sandwiches or subs, with meats, cheese and often a fried egg, and conkies (sometimes kankis) which are real Bajan fast food. They consist of a mixture of corn meal, coconut, pumpkin, sweet potatoes, raisins and spices which are wrapped inside a banana leaf and steamed.

cooked very slowly to make cheaper cuts of meat as tender as possible. In the old days the meager meat ration would be supplemented by ground provisions.

Rice and peas or beans are usually served as accompaniments to main meals, although you may be offered green bananas, fried plantain or sweet potatoes. Some restaurants serve macaroni cheese as a side dish.

Other dishes

As a reminder of English cooking, you might be offered souse, a delicious meat stew in which lots of unmentionable bits from the pig are used, including head and tail, together with peppers and onions, lime and cucumbers. Traditional English savory puddings, both black and white, are also served although ingredients have been adapted so that local produce can be used. Black pudding consists of grated sweet potatoes, shallots and spices, all mixed with pig's blood, and then stuffed into a pig's intestine and boiled. It may not sound an appealing recipe, but slices of fried black pudding are delicious, especially for breakfast. White pudding has the same ingredients without the blood. Boiled puddings

pepper pot. Meat is put in the pot, casareep, peppers and spices are added and the liquid is then brought to the boil. Provided the liquid is brought to the boil each day, the meat retains its freshness, and as some of the contents of the pot are eaten, new ingredients can be added. It is said that some of the island's pepper pots, contents and all, have been passed down through several generations and are still in use.

There are lots of other stews and casseroles which were traditionally

Caution – hot pepper sauce!

On most tables you will find a bottle of pepper sauce. It usually contains a blend of several types of hot pepper, spices and vinegar, and should be treated cautiously. Try a little first before splashing it all over your food, as these sauces range from hot to unbearable.

If you want to make your own hot pepper sauce, take four ripe hot peppers, one teaspoon each of oil and vinegar and a pinch of salt, blend together into a liquid, and bottle.

River Bay

Enjoy a cocktail at Crystal Cove

are traditionally served on Saturday nights for dinner.

There are curries which were brought to the islands by Indian laborers in the mid-19th century, and are delicious. They can feature chicken, lamb or goat.

Accompaniments

There are wonderful fresh fruit juices, and the fruit is also used to make tasty desserts which often include soursop ice cream or sapodilla pudding. Try star apple, soursop, sapodilla, pineapple and mango, or fresh pawpaw (papaya) sliced with a squeeze of lime juice. The Barbados cherry has the highest concentration of vitamin C of any fruit in the world. There are also coconut cakes, guava cheese and pastries.

Sweet potato is often served with fish and meat instead of potatoes, yellow yam is also served as a potato substitute and has a nutty flavor. Many fruits are also traditionally served with meats. Many cakes and puddings also feature ginger.

DRINK

Yo, ho, ho and a bottle of rum

Columbus is credited with planting the first sugar cane in the Caribbean, on Hispaniola, during his third voyage, and the Spanish called it *aguardiente de cana*, meaning cane liquor. The Latin name for sugar cane is *saccharum*, and it was English sailors who shortened this to rum. A more colorful suggestion is that the name comes from the old English word 'rumbullion'. In English this meant a drunken brawl but it more likely comes from the Dutch word for the large drinking glass it was consumed in. In any event, one of the earliest recorded references to the word was in 1650 when it was used to describe the main drink on the island. It was also affectionately known as 'kill-devil' because it was so strong that people drinking it were 'quickly laid out on the ground in a deep sleep'.

The first rum on Barbados was produced at least 350 years ago and became an important international commodity. It was, and many say still is, the finest rum available, and was exported throughout the Caribbean, to North America and England. It figured prominently in the infamous Triangle Trade in which slaves from Africa were sold for rum from the West Indies which was sold to raise money to buy more slaves.

Rum had such fortifying powers that General George Washington insisted every soldier be given a daily ration, and a daily tot also became a tradition in the British Royal Navy. The very strong Navy Rum was a blend containing rum from Barbados, and the daily tot was dispensed until 1970.

Barbados rum is still considered one of the world's finest, and there are those who say it is the best. There are three distilleries on the island producing rum and rum products, and all can be visited and their wares tasted and purchased. These are Mount Gay, the West India Rum Refinery (Hanschell Inniss), and the new **Rum Factory**, the first to be built on the island this century.

The Mount Gay Distillery can be visited in St Lucy as well as the bottling and blending plant just outside Bridgetown. There are also Wednesday tours with lunch to the **West India Rum Refinery**, Black Rock (☎ 425-9393), home of Cockspur rum and Malibu, a drink made from white rum and coconut.

All sorts of rums are produced from light to dark and of varying strengths. Rum is aged in American white oak barrels, and the longer it remains in the barrel, the more flavor and color it absorbs. Traditionally, dark rum spent a long time aging in barrels, and light rums only a short time. Today, most white and light rums are not aged in wood, but in stainless steel vats.

The **rum shop** is an island institution – there are believed to be more than 1,500. It is the place for the men to hang out, especially on Sunday morning when the ladies are at church. Rum is also so interwoven with island life and tradition, that it is drunk on all important occasions, such as births, weddings and funerals. It can be drunk neat, on the rocks, with a little water, or with any mixer you prefer. It is even sprinkled around a house to keep duppies away.

Soft drinks

Rum features in many of the island's most popular cocktails, but there are many excellent local soft drinks as well, such as the freshest fruit juices and fruit punches. Mauby, sometimes maubi, is made from boiling a bitter tree bark and then mixing the liquid with herbs and spices. It is then sweetened to taste. The mauby lady used to be a familiar sight on the streets of Bridgetown, but is no more although the drink is still available. Other drinks include freshly made lemonade and delicious old-style ginger beer. Nonalcoholic malt drinks are also popular. There are also many different sorts of herbal and fruit teas, such as sorrel, which make great thirst quenchers and revivers.

Beer

Banks beer and Jubilee ale are brewed on the island. There are tours of **Banks Brewery** on Tuesday and Thursday (☎ 429-2113).

Cocktails

Planter's Punch

Combine 2 ounces (56g) each of pineapple juice, rum, cream of coconut and half an ounce (14g) of lime in a blender for one minute. Pour into a chilled glass, add a sprinkle of coconut shavings and garnish with a cherry and a slice of orange.

Barbados Rum Punch

An easy way of remembering the recipe is to recall an old West Indian saying which goes: 'one of sour, two of sweet, three of strong, and four of weak'.

Mix one part lime or lemon juice, two parts of syrup, three parts of rum and four parts of water or fruit juice. Pour over crushed ice, sprinkle with nutmeg and add a slice of lime, lemon or a wedge of pineapple. The punch is even better if prepared and allowed to 'mature' for 24 hours.

*B*arbados has an extensive road network with almost 1,000 miles (1,600km) of highway and almost all of it is paved, although the surface condition varies enormously. If you plan to do a lot of exploring, and there are lots of things to see and do, car rental is the best option. If you plan to spend most of your time in and around your resort, it is better to take a bus, rent a taxi for occasional touring, or go on an organized trip. Many large hotels and resorts operate their own shuttle buses into town. Motor scooters and bicycles are also available for hire.

GETTING AROUND

Buses

Barbados Transport Board buses operate throughout the island. They are painted blue with a yellow stripe. There is a timetable and on the front of each bus there is a destination board telling you where it is going – assuming the driver has changed it! Buses are very good value although you may have to wait for the right bus to come along. They do provide a fun way of getting around and an excellent opportunity to get to meet the Bajans. The buses are generally packed during the long rush hour periods (7-10am and 4-7pm), especially around Bridgetown when traffic often comes to a complete standstill.

There are Transport Board bus stations at: Fairchild Street, Bridgetown (☎ 427-8795) mainly for the south and east; Jubilee, Lower Green, Bridgetown (☎ 426-5694) for the north via the west coast; Princess Alice Highway, Bridgetown (☎ 426-2832), Mangrove Depot, St Philip (☎ 435-5440), Haggatts Depot, St Andrew (☎ 422-9117); and Speightstown (☎ 422-2410). For information on routes call any of the bus terminals or the Transport Board Headquarters at Weymouth, Roebuck Street, Bridgetown (☎ 436-6820).

One advantage of bus travel is that there is a set fare of Bsd$1.50 whatever the destination but you must have the exact fare. You can also buy tokens at bus stations if you plan to do a lot of bus travel. Buses are only allowed to pick up and drop off at authorized bus stops, you cannot just flag them down. Bus stops are usually marked 'To Town' or 'Out of Town' which helps. There are also some excellent island bus tours which pick you up and then return you to your hotel.

Mini-buses

Mini-buses and Route Taxi mini-buses are privately owned, and usually bear the 'street name' of the driver in bold lettering. Mini-buses are painted yellow with a blue stripe, have ZR on their number plates, and operate along set routes, mostly the busiest ones, and charge the same Bsd$1.50 fare. This form of transport is a great way to meet the locals but is not for the faint hearted as the drivers race along in order to pick up the maximum number of passengers in the short-est possible time. Avoid rush hour travel when the buses are packed and always check where they are going before getting on.

In Bridgetown mini-buses operate from the River Bus Terminal (☎ 426-3967) for Bayfield, Bush Hall, Crane, Dash Valley via Government Hill and Mapp Hill, Ellerton via Salters or Walkers, Greens via Salters, Pine via Wildey, Sugar Hill, St Patrick's and St John's Parish Church via Four Cross Roads. From Temple Yard, Cheapside there are buses to the central and eastern parts of the island – Belleplaine, Boscobelle, Cave Hill, Checker Hall, Deacons Road and Grazettes, Eden Lodge, Holder's Green, Holder's Hill, Jackson, Speightstown and Sturges. From the Probyn Street terminal there are mini-buses to Flagstaff, Gall Hill, Oistins, Pine, Rendevouz and Silver Hill.

There are also privately owned maxi-taxis, recognized by a mauve stripe. They have set routes and again the fare is Bds$1.50.

Taxis

These are reasonably priced, especially if sharing, widely available, and recognized by the letter Z on the license plate.

Taxis are not metered and you should always agree on the price of a ride before setting off. You should also make sure what currency is being quoted – US or Barbados dollars – to avoid any misunderstandings.

There are taxis at most hotels and taxi stands at Accra Beach and Hastings Rocks on the south coast, at Sunset Crest Shopping Centres I and II on the west coast, at the international airport, and in Bridgetown at Independence Square, Lower Broad Street and Trafalgar Square. Typical fares from the airport to: Speightstown Bsd$50, Bridgetown Harbour Bsd$30, Crane Bsd$20, St Lawrence Bsd$20 and Callenders Bsd$16. From Bridgetown expect the fare to the following destinations to be about: East Point Bsd$40, St John's Parish Church Bsd$36, Long Beach Bsd$24, Rendevouz Bsd$16, and Paradise Bsd$12.

Taxi drivers generally are very friendly and very knowledgeable about the island and make excellent tour guides. Taxis can be hired for half day or day tours. Expect to pay around Bsd$30-35 an hour or around Bds$200-240 for a day's tour, depending on how good you are at negotiating the best deal and how long you plan to be out.

Car rental

A car, often a mini moke, offers the best way of exploring the island at your own pace. Have a good road map as many roads are not well signposted, and always plan on taking longer to get to your destination that the distance alone might suggest. Drive on the left and drive carefully. There are potholes, blind corners, and roundabouts on which you yield to all traffic on your right. Observe the speed limits even if others do not. Some

Bajans are quite likely to stop in the middle of the road to chat or even pop into a shop causing a long queue of traffic. If it happens accept it stoically.

By air

There are a number of small airports and airstrips around the island and it is possible to charter small aircraft to fly from one area to another, or to take an aerial tour, or visit neighboring islands. **Bajan Helicopters** (☎ 431-0069) also offer island tours.

By submarine

Atlantis Submarines offer Submarine and Seatrec trips. The Seatrec is a unique reef observation craft that allows passengers to sit in comfort six feet below the surface as it cruises over coral, tropical fish and the wreck of the *Lord Willoughby*. They are based in the Shallow Draft, Bridgetown (☎ 436-8929).

Money Saving Tip

The Barbados Heritage Passport will save you money if you plan to do a lot of sightseeing. If you pay full admission at four Heritage sites, you get free admission to four others.

• BRIDGETOWN •

*B*ridgetown was founded by sixty-four settlers, led by Charles Wolverstone, sent out by the Earl of Carlisle in 1628, and got its name because there was an Indian bridge across the waterway, now known as the Constitution River. Early names included Indian Bridge and The Bridge, before finally becoming Bridgetown. Carlisle is honored by the bay named after him on which Bridgetown lies. The settlement was established because of the suitability of Carlisle Bay as an anchorage and settlers did not appreciate the dangers of the nearby swamp and the mosquitoes that spread yellow fever and malaria.

The Carenage with St Michael's Cathedral and the Parliament Buildings in the backgound

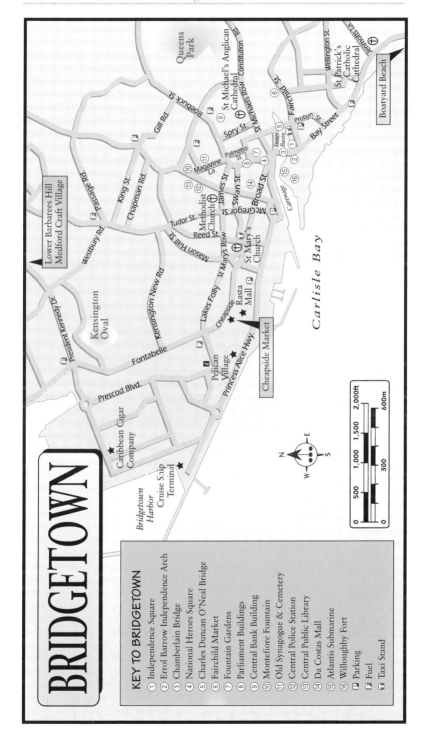

BRIDGETOWN

KEY TO BRIDGETOWN

1. Independence Square
2. Errol Barrow Independence Arch
3. Chamberlain Bridge
4. National Heroes Square
5. Charles Duncan O'Neal Bridge
6. Fairchild Market
7. Fountain Gardens
8. Parliament Buildings
9. Central Bank Building
10. Montefiore Fountain
11. Old Synagogue & Cemetery
12. Central Police Station
13. Central Public Library
14. Da Costas Mall
15. Atlantis Submarine
16. Willoughby Fort
P. Parking
F. Fuel
T. Taxi Stand

It is the main town, the island's only sea port and the administrative, shopping, commercial and artistic capital of the island. Almost forty per cent of the island's 255,000 population live in or close to Bridgetown, and a network of eight major roads fan out from the capital providing easy access to all parts of the island.

One fascinating feature of Bridgetown is that it retains many of its original street names, because these were enshrined in an Act of Parliament passed in 1657. Broad Street, now Bridgetown's main street, used to be called Cheapside, and is still called that by some of the islanders.

Bridgetown has been hit many times over the years by hurricanes and fires. In 1657, fire swept through most of the city, and in 1675 a hurricane destroyed much of Bridgetown, as it did again in 1780, when thousands lost their lives.

A WALKING TOUR

National Heroes Square (see below), formerly Trafalgar Square, beside the Carenage makes a good place to start a walking tour of Bridgetown.

The **War Memorial** in the square is dedicated to the many Barbadians who lost their lives fighting in the two World Wars, and the **Fountain Gardens** at the eastern end of the square, is visited later in the tour.

The busy **Carenage** gets its name because in the old days, ships would be beached here and then rolled on their sides so that their hulls could be repaired and cleared of barnacles. This process was known as careening. The Carenage is now a busy little marina surrounded by popular and lively nightspots.

Broad Street has been the main shopping street for 300 years, and its most famous landmark is the

National Heroes Square' origin

The square, formerly called Eggington's Green, was then named in 1806 in honor of Admiral Lord Horatio Nelson who died at the Battle of Trafalgar on 21 October 1805. Nelson and his fleet gathered in Carlisle Bay in July of 1805 not knowing that a combined fleet of French and Spanish ships were planning to attack the island. When the enemy fleet saw the British war ships, however, they sailed away. News of Nelson's great victory – and death – off Cape Trafalgar arrived in December.

The statue of Nelson, sculpted by Sir William Westmacott, was erected in 1813, many years before Nelson's Column was completed in London's Trafalgar Square. Originally Nelson faced out to sea, but during a redevelopment the statue was turned and now faces inland. The square was improved following a fire in 1860 that damaged many of the surrounding buildings. In 1999, the name changed again to National Heroes Square.

impressive 1895 Mutual Life Assurance Building with its twin white domes. It runs off Trafalgar Square. **Swan Street** that runs parallel with it is also packed with fascinating shops and bazaars.

Walk over the **Chamberlain Bridge** that separates The Carenage and the **Inner Basin**. There have been many wooden bridges over the centuries, and most have been washed away by hurricanes, floodwater or burnt down. The swingbridge was opened on 18 April 1872 but seriously damaged by a hurricane in 1898. Repairs took two years and it was re-opened in 1900 by Lady Hay, the Governor's wife. It was later named the Chamberlain Bridge, after Joseph Chamberlain, the British Colonial Secretary, who approved massive grant aid that salvaged the island's devastated economy.

Looking inland from the Chamberlain Bridge you can see the **Charles Duncan O'Neal Bridge**, although it is still often referred to as Victoria Bridge. The wooden Victoria Bridge was replaced by an iron structure at the beginning of the 20th century. This was dismantled in 1967 and replaced by the present structure named after one of the island's founding fathers of democracy.

The **Fairchild Market** is over the bridge and close to the bustling bus terminal. The market is busy most weekdays but especially on Sunday. It sells local produce, some arts and crafts, T-shirts and tourist goods.

On the eastern side of Chamberlain Bridge is the splendid **Errol Barrow Independence Arch** and beyond there are the old warehouses built close to the pier, on land that was once used to graze cattle. The warehouses are now the home of nightclubs and restaurants and offices. **Willoughby Fort** near the pier, was built on Little Island in 1656. Landfill has connected it to the mainland, and it is now the headquarters of the Coast Guard.

The Independence Arch was built in 1987 to celebrate the island's 21st anniversary of independence. Under the arches are portraits of Errol Walton Barrow, the late Prime Minister and the man who led the country to independence in 1966.

Cross Independence Square to Probyn Street and then turn left to cross the Charles Duncan O'Neal Bridge into Bridge Street to visit the **Fountain Gardens** on your left at the eastern end of National Heroes Square.

Foutain Gardens

Bridgetown received its first piped drinking water in 1860 and a year later, an editorial in the Barbadian newspaper, said that it would be a good idea to commemorate that by erecting a fountain. The idea caught on, a public fund was launched and in 1865 the ornate fountain arrived in Barbados. It was officially unveiled by the Acting Governor Major Robert Mundy in July as an artillery salute was fired and the bells of St Michael's Cathedral chimed. Work on the formal gardens, however, did not start until 1882.

Above: Independence Arch

Left: Fountain Gardens

Below: The Carenage

Above: Chamberlin bridge

Right: Bethel Church

Below: Synagogue Lane

From Fountain Gardens cross over the road to visit the **Parliament Buildings**, the third oldest in the English speaking world. The Parliament was founded in 1637 and has met regularly since 1639. The present buildings, built of coral stone quarried on the island, date from the 1870s. The West Building was completed in 1871 and the East Building three years later.

Looking out over National Heroes Square and the Chamberlain Bridge, the magnificent Italian-Renaissance buildings house both the House of Assembly and Senate Chamber. The stained glass windows in the East Building depict British monarchs from King James I to Queen Victoria, and even Oliver Cromwell is portrayed. The carved Speaker's Chair was an Independence gift from India. A statue of Sir William Conrad, the island's first black Chief Justice stands in the front of the legislature.

From the public buildings walk along St Michael's Row to visit **St Michael's Anglican Cathedral**. The first church on the site was consecrated in 1665, replacing a small wooden structure, and was destroyed in the 1780 hurricane. The present edifice dates from 1789, and became a cathedral in 1825 with William Hart Coleridge, nephew of poet Samuel Taylor Coleridge, its first Bishop.

It is noted for its huge arched roof, at one time the widest in the world, and the 1680 font with its Greek palindrome inscription, which means 'wash the sin, not only the skin'. The churchyard contains the tombs of many of the island's most famous sons and daughters, and garrison soldiers, some in their teens, who died of disease. Behind the cathedral is Cathedral Square and the Masonic Temple, formerly the Harrison's Free School founded in 1733 to educate the children of the poor.

From the cathedral retrace your route to Spry Street past the massive **Central Bank Building**. The 11-floor tower block is the highest in Barbados, and the headquarters of the Central Bank of Barbados and the Barbados Development Bank. It is also home of the 500-seat Frank Collymore Hall, the island's premier concert hall, named after the noted Barbadian poet, actor and teacher.

At the end of Spry Street turn left into Roebuck Street and proceed until it joins Palmetto Street. Keep

Jewish influence in Barbados

The Jewish community has played an important role in the community since the founding of the island's first settlement. The first Jews arrived in the 1620s from Brazil, and they helped introduce sugar cane to the island.

The original synagogue dates from 1654 following the settlement of a colony of Dutch Jews from Brazil. It is the oldest in the Western Hemisphere. It was partly destroyed by a hurricane in 1831 but rebuilt and re-dedicated in 1833. The synagogue ceased to be used in 1926 and was sold as offices. In the 1980s, however, the local right for a short distance to Synagogue Lane and the **Old Synagogue** and **Cemetery**.

From Synagogue Lane turn left into Magazine Lane, and then left again into Pinfold to its junction with Coleridge Street, to view the **Montefiore Fountain**, another reminder of the Jewish presence on the island. The drinking fountain, presented to the city of Bridgetown by John Montefiore in memory of his father, was originally sited in Beckwith Place in 1865. It was moved to its present location in Coleridge Street in 1940, on the green opposite the Law Courts and the **Central Public Library**, a gift from Andrew Carnegie in 1906. The library is open from 9am to 5pm Monday to Saturday (☎ 426-1744) and is worth a visit because it has a fine collection of old books

Jewish community bought back the building and restored it.

The Jewish Cemetery stands next door and contains many interesting tombstones, the oldest dating back to 1630s. The square two-story white synagogue has recently been restored. It has a remarkable symmetry with its flat parapet roof and ornamental work over the windows. It is open to the public between 9am and 4pm Monday to Friday (☎ 426-5792). As you approach the synagogue is the old school house which is being restored into the Synagogue Library.

and newspapers about Barbados which can be inspected.

Head back into town along Coleridge Street past the **Central Police Station**, and then turn right into James Street past the **Methodist Church**.

The first Methodist missionaries arrived on the island in 1788 with the aim of educating the slaves and 'bringing them to God'. This idea proved so horrific to the landowners that they barred the missionaries from the plantations, and the Methodists for many years were effectively restricted to Bridgetown. In 1823 the Methodist Church was deliberately destroyed but the missionaries persevered, and by the time of Emancipation their following had grown and there were a number of churches throughout the island.

Continue over the junction to St Mary's Row, past **St Mary's Church**, built in 1827 when the congregations at St Michael's became too large, to the **Cheapside Market**, the town's second market. It sells produce, both locally grown and imported by boat from St Vincent. It also sells some tourist items and souvenirs. The **Rasta Mall** is south of Cheapside market and sells a wide range of Rastafarian goods, both spiritual and secular.

Then follow the road as it becomes Lakes Folly until it connects with Princess Alice Highway that runs along the bay. Turn right for **Bridgetown Harbor** and the modern **Cruise Ship Terminal** with its duty-free shops, information center and banking facilities.

The deepwater harbor was opened in 1961 after four years of

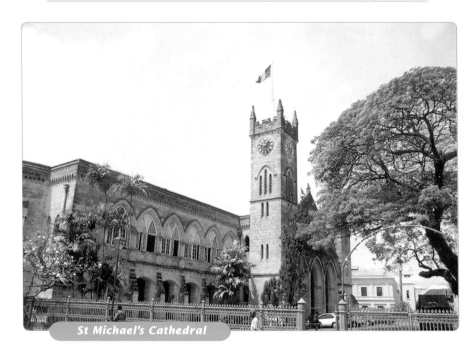

St Michael's Cathedral

Bridgetown Harbor

dredging, landfill and construction incorporating Pelican Island, once the home of large numbers of brown pelicans. The island now houses offices and the giant wedge-shaped sugar warehouse. There are more than a score of duty-free shops offering the world's finest jewelry, clothing, china, cameras and electronic equipment. In particular, check out the work of local designers.

After visiting the terminal, you can stroll back along the waterfront to visit the **Pelican Village**, an arts and crafts center in beautifully landscaped gardens. Established by the Industrial Development Corporation, the village is home to many of the island's best artists and craftsmen. You can watch them at work and buy their wares, and then walk back along the Esplanade to the town center.

OTHER THINGS TO SEE AND DO

Markets & malls

Visit the two covered street markets in Fairchild Street and Cheapside. Both sell a wide range of island produce. If you are interested in shopping, also visit the **Bridgetown Mall** and **Da Costas Mall** both off Broad Street.

Queen's Park

Queen's Park is beyond St Michael's Cathedral off Constitution Road. The park was formerly the official residence of the General commanding the British troops in the West Indies, and before Queen

Atlantis Subarine

Victoria came to the throne was known as King's House. When the British troops left at the beginning of this century, the land was taken over by the then Vestry of St Michael and turned into a park, which opened on 10 June 1909. It is now run by the National Conservation Commission and is being restored to its former glory.

The grounds contain a giant baobab tree with a girth of just over 61 feet (18m) which is believed to the largest tree on the island. The tree is thought to be at least 1,000 years old, and as it is a native of West Africa, it is a mystery how it came to be growing on Barbados hundreds of years before the first African slaves arrived.

St Patrick's Catholic Cathedral

The cathedral is on the southern outskirts of the town, just beyond the junction of Jemmotts Lane and Bay Street which continues as highway 7 past the Fish Market. Because the Church of England was the official religion on the island – with Anglican clergy paid for by the state – Catholicism was virtually outlawed. An Act of 1650 stipulated that the only worship allowed was the Anglican religion.

Many Irish Catholics were 'Barbadosed' by Cromwell, and Catholic priests accompanying them, were either refused permission to land, imprisoned or put to work themselves. It was not until 1839 that the Catholic Church was officially recognized on Barbados with the appointment of a Bishop to the West Indies, based in Trinidad. The cathedral's corner stone was laid on 24 December

1840, but because of the island's small Catholic population and lack of funds, the church was not completed until nine years later.

The church was destroyed by fire on 13 June 1887 and the present building was completed in 1899 with subscriptions from Government, Catholic Church, Protestant and Jewish communities. On 18 March 1970, the Bishopric of Bridgetown and Kingstown (St Vincent) was created, and the church was elevated to the status of cathedral.

The National Stadium

The staduim was opened by Prince Charles in 1970 and has a seating capacity of 5,000 with standing room for a further 1,000. It hosts many of the island's major events and features prominently in the Crop Over Festival.

The Medford Craft Village

Based at Lower Barbarees Hill, it is just 3 miles (5km) from Bridgetown and the only place on the island where you can watch craftsmen working with enormous slabs of mahogany weighing up to 4 tons. The village, created by self-taught artist Reggie Medford, is set among mahogany trees and you can watch them working and visit their private showroom. It is open daily (☎ 427-3179).

The Caribbean Cigar Company

The company welcomes visitors and you can watch the finest hand made cigars being made from Cuban tobacco. Their most famous brands are Sam Lord and Royal Barbados Cigars. The factory is about five minutes from the port on Harbour Road. There are factory tours (☎ 437-8519).

The Atlantis Submarine

Offers an underwater trip along the west coast. The tender leaves Bridgetown every hour from 9am to 8pm for the 15 minute journey out to Atlantis II and the dive site, the world's first recreational submarine. It seats 48 passengers – 24 on either side who sit looking out through large portholes. There is an even larger window – 52 feet (16m) – in front.

The underwater trip lasts almost one hour and the tender remains above and in radio contact at all times. The submarine dives to 130 feet (40m) and cruises over coral reefs and alongside the wreck of the *Lord Willoughby*. Lighting conditions are suitable for both still and video photography. There are hourly dives during the day from Monday to Saturday and night dives (☎ 436-8929).

The Sherbourne Center

The centre is the island's modern international conference center and facility with 1,000 theatre-seat auditorium, exhibition halls, restaurant, lounges and secretarial facilities, and conveniently situated opposite the Caribbean Broadcasting Union overlooking the St George Valley, bordering Ilaro Court. It is also the venue for the twice-weekly dinner show, '*1627 And All That*'.

Eating out in and around Bridgetown

The **Balcony Café**, Cave Shepherd, is a first floor open-air cafe overlooking bustling Broad Street, and offering breakfast, lunch, snacks and afternoon drinks. It is noted for its rum punches. The store's top floor **Ideal Restaurant** serves Bajan specialties and fresh baked items.

Fisherman's Wharf and the **Waterfront Café**, both on the Carenage offer Bajan and seafood dishes. There are a number of food kiosks in **Da Costas Mall**, good salad bars at the **Barbeque Barn** and **Barbados Pizza House** on Broad Street, and the **Ly Jing Restaurant**, which overlooks Broad Street, and offers both Chinese and Caribbean cooking. **Mustor's** on McGregor Street is noted for its traditional Bajan country fare. (See also list at end of this section).

• ISLAND TOURS •

*T*he following tours are suggested to take in all the sights of interest. Because of the layout of secondary and even smaller side roads, it is not always possible to drive directly from one place to another, and a certain amount of weaving to and from is required. By following signs and tracing your route on a good map, and taking your time, your will ensure to get to see all that there is, and more. And if you do get lost the chances are that a Bajan will stop and give you directions.

Rockley Beach

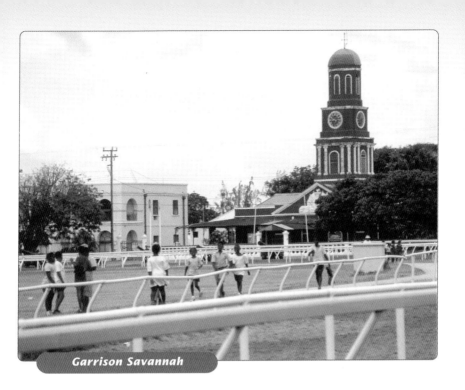

Garrison Savannah

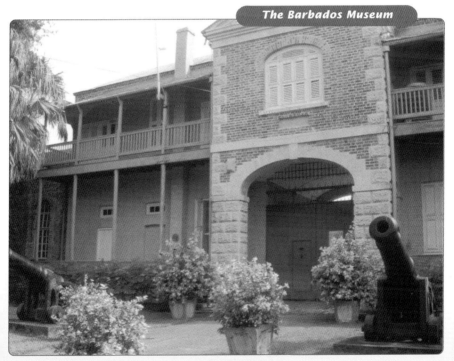

The Barbados Museum

THE SOUTHERN TOUR

O ur tour heads south from Bridgetown to travel round the southern half of the island in an anti-clockwise direction. It follows close to the coastline using both main roads and secondary roads, with frequent suggestions for detours inland.

The tour starts on highway 7, the South Coast Road, which runs through the sprawling suburbs along Carlisle Bay, past the exclusive Harbour Lights open-air night club, with live entertainment most nights.

Of interest is **Crofton's House** at the junction of Bay Street and Chelsea Road, which is where George Washington is alleged to have stayed in the mid-1750s.

With the Bay Estate on your left, continue to **Garrison Savannah**, the original garrison which is now used as a race track. This is an historic Garrison area as it was the first garrison in the West Indies and probably in the whole of North America. It is now the home of the **Barbados Museum** and contains many fine old buildings, forts and monuments inland, as well as Needham's Point and the St Ann's Fort and Barracks, the headquarters of the Barbados Defence Forces, on the seaward side to your right. You will also spot the oil refinery.

Charles Fort, originally Needham's Fort, was built in the 1650s on Needham's Point when it was feared that a Commonwealth force sent by Oliver Cromwell might try to invade island. It was the first of more than 50 forts built around the island.

To the east is **St Ann's Fort**, built after war broke out between England and France in 1688. Most of the other garrison buildings date from 1789 when Britain decided to make Barbados the headquarters for its military forces in the Windward and Leeward Islands. Eventually the garrison covered 150 acres and contained more than 70 buildings. The **Military Cemetery** is also here and the tombstones bear testimony to the hardships endured by many of the soldiers and their families. The cemetery, which had fallen into neglect, has now been restored and it is now both a tranquil area and a historically fascinating one. Close by is the Barbados Museum (see opposite).

Just down the road from the museum on the beach by the Barbados Hilton, is **Dive Boat Safari**, a dive shop, which offers a wide range of watersports and diving activities including reef and wreck dives. Five-day courses take complete novices to PADI and NAUI certification.

The tour then continues along the coast to **Hastings** with its famed Ile de France French restaurant, and the Sandy Bank Beach Bar and Restaurant which claims to be 'the brightest, bluest, bestest bar on the south coast'. This is a salad bar and an open-air grill bar with

The museum was once the military prison. Built around 1818, it offers a fascinating insight into the history and culture of the island. Many of the former garrison buildings are now offices or splendid private homes. Work continues on restoring the garrison, and in particular the **National Cannon Collection**, the largest collection of 17th century English cannon in the world.

The Barbados Museum is a must, and the earlier in your stay you visit the better as it gives a wonderful overview about the island, its history, natural history, culture and people. The museum was founded in 1933 by a group of people who got together to buy a collection of shells, fossils and other natural history specimens in order to preserve them for posterity.

St Ann's Garrison provides a unique setting for the museum, which is housed in the former military prison built with limestone and yellow brick in 1820 – a fine example of West Indies Georgian architecture. The exhibits are in galleries, many of which used to be small cells holding prisoners.

The marble fountain near the entrance used to be outside the Bridgetown Synagogue so that worshippers could wash their hands before entering. Access is through the gift shop, but leave browsing here until you have visited the museum.

Exhibits in the **Harewood Gallery** include displays about the island's natural history, both on land and in the water. The **Jubilee Gallery** concentrates on the island's history, with exhibits dating back to pre-Columbian times and the Amerindians. There are many fine exhibits including a large shell which has been inscribed with the Lord's Prayer, some wonderful old maps, in the **Cunard Gallery**, as well as prints, paintings, guidebooks and a copy of the Barbados Mercury dated 22 July 1789.

Other galleries have recreated rooms to reflect the comfortable lifestyle of planters on the island in the 19th century, displays of militaria, African musical instruments, sculptures and woodcarvings. There is also a fine collection of late 18th century glass, ceramics, silver and furniture, and a delightful children's gallery with hands-on exhibits and displays.

The museum's excellent research library is also available to interested parties, and is open from 10am to 1pm, Monday to Friday. The museum is open Monday to Saturday 9am to 5pm and 2pm to 6pm Sunday (☎ 427-0201). Every Thursday the museum presents a buffet dinner and the lavish '1627 And All That' show. You can go just for the show, if you prefer (☎ 428-1627).

The **Garrison Historic Area** has buildings dating from the mid-17th century, many of which housed the British Garrison stationed there from 1780 until 1905. Part of the **National Canon Collection** is on display in front of the Main Guard building with its prominent clock tower, and contains many rare cannon. Unlike almost every other Caribbean island, Barbados was never invaded because it was so difficult to attack and so well fortified. The collection when complete, will contain the largest collection of 17th century cannon in the world, including a very rare Commonwealth gun, which is stamped with the arms of Cromwell. Only one other similar cannon is known to exist.

Also visit the **Mallalieu Motor Collection** at Pavilion Court. It is open daily and at any time by appointment (☎ 426-4640).

an inspired list of cocktails and shooters, including their famous Jello shots. It is always lively (☎ 435-6689).

You should also visit the **Shell Gallery**, one of the finest shell shops in the Caribbean with a fantastic collection from around the world. The gallery also sells shell jewelry and shell art by Maureen Edghill, whose works have been presented to Queen Elizabeth.

The next stretch of coast road is also through built up areas such as **Worthing** with its small beach and many small guesthouses. Along this stretch of coastline from Bridgetown there are many fine beaches, restaurants and shops.

Inland from Worthing is the **Graeme Hall Swamp and Bird Sanctuary**, the largest stretch of inland water on the island, and a mecca for bird watchers. The man-grove tree-lines swamp hosts native birds as well as large numbers of migrants and winter visitors.

Also inland off highway 6 near **Clapham** is the **Harry Bayley Observatory**, the headquarters of the Barbados Astronomical Society that was founded in 1956. The observatory, which opened in 1963, is the only one in the Caribbean. It has a 14 inch (36cm) reflector telescope. It is open every Friday evening from 8.30pm to 11.30pm. There is a small admission charge.

North of the observatory is **The Aquatic Centre** with its Olympic-size pool that opened in 1990. It is the venue for national and international swimming events and water polo. It is part of a sports complex that includes the **Sir Garfield Sobers Sports Complex**, opened in 1992, with 4,000-seat gymnasium, tennis, hockey and football fields.

Worthing

Chattel House Village, St Lawrence Gap

The urban sprawl continues all along the coast as far as Oistins. Our route turns off the main road on to the St Lawrence Coast Road that leads to the **St Lawrence Gap**. Here you can visit Tapps Tavern and Grill that serves delicious food cooked before your eyes, good music, and has more happy hours each day than any other bar I know. It is also the home of the world famous 'Shooter Chair', a reclining chair that allows you to throw back 'shots' of spirits with much greater ease!

Two other musts are the Chattel House Village and the Coffee and Cream Art Gallery. The **Chattel House Village** is a fascinating collection of shops built in the style of typical servant cottages or chattel houses. In the center of the courtyard is the **Biddy's Information Centre** that can help you plan your trip in the area. Surrounding the courtyard are a collection of delightful mini-shops offering everything from tropical fashions to hand-crafted souvenirs, and delicious exotic ice creams to home-made jewelry. There is also the inevitable rum shop.

The **Coffee and Cream Art Gallery** (☎ 428-2708), in Paradise Village off Marine Lane, offers the finest collection of constantly changing original art on the island. Owners Darla and David Trotman have done a tremendous amount to encourage and promote many of the island's most talented artists. Apart from paintings, there are sculptures, pottery, elaborately woven baskets, wood carvings and hand-made and hand-crafted jewelry. After browsing and deciding what you should buy, you can enjoy a drink on the verandah.

If you want to shop or enjoy a range of cuisines, head inland for the **Sheraton Centre** in Sargeant's Village, which is about ten minutes from the Gap. The Centre boasts more than 75 shops, boutiques and eateries and many of the stores offer duty-free shopping.

From St Lawrence take the Maxwell Top Road to **Oistins**, a charming but busy fishing village that has seen a lot of changes in recent years. Oistins was named after Edward Oistin, the original plantation owner.

It is now the island's main fishing port and with Government funds, a modern jetty and cold stores have been built, the fish market expanded and additional car parking provided. In the old days, when there was a large fish catch, it all had to be sold because there were no storage facilities, and by the time the last boxes were offered for sale, prices had fallen through the floor. Now when the colorful fishing boats return with a big catch, the initial demand can be met, and any surplus frozen for those days when the boats cannot go to sea, or when the catch is very low.

Oistins is also famous because in the early days of the island's settlement, this was where the Royalist and Roundhead camps finally hammered out a peace pact, the Articles of Agreement or Charter of Barbados as it became known, which led to Barbados accepting the authority of Cromwell. The agreement was thrashed out and signed in the Mermaid Tavern in 1652.

There are some wonderful old buildings in the village, many of them rum shops, and many of these listed as preserved buildings.

On the hill to the east of Oistins is **Christ Church Parish Church**. It dates from 1935 and is the fifth church to be built in the parish, the others having been destroyed by flood, fire or hurricane over the last 300 years.

Chase Vault

In the churchyard is the Chase Vault, the subject of a long running mystery. Although the vault has always been sealed, the very heavy lead-lined coffins repeatedly changed position. In 1812 when the vault was opened so that the body of Colonel Thomas Chase could be placed inside, all the coffins were found to be out of place. They were returned to their original positions and the vault securely sealed but again in 1816 and 1817, the same thing happened.

As horror stories spread through the island, the Governor ordered the vault to be opened again and inspected. In 1819 he personally supervised the examination. The coffins which were strewn about as before, were put back in their proper positions, and the vault secured yet again with the Governor's seal impressed in cement on the vault wall.

In 1820 when the vault was next checked, all the coffins were out of position again. The family decided that enough was enough, and they ordered all the coffins to be removed and buried separately at plots in the churchyard.

From Oistins you can take a small detour along the coast road that runs round **Cotton House Bay** and then cuts past the unique **South Point Lighthouse**, which is the only structure on the island built completely of cast iron. The lighthouse was made in England and exhibited at the Great Exhibition in London's Hyde Park in 1851. When the exhibition closed, the lighthouse was taken down in June and shipped in sections to Barbados. It was fully operational by April 1852.

Continue to **Silver Sands** and the Silver Rock Hotel at **Little Bay**. This area is very popular with windsurfers and the Silver Rock restaurant and bar is usually a lively place. The world windsurfing championships have been held here, and the conditions make it suitable for intermediate and advanced windsurfers. Windsurfing equipment can be rented and expert instructors are available. It is also a good place for body surfing.

The tour continues, however, on highway 7 that runs east through **Calendar** and north of the **Grantley Adams International Airport**. The airport, with its Canadian-designed concrete-sculpted terminal building, is one of the most modern in the Caribbean and its long runway can accommodate the largest jets, as well as Concorde that is a regular winter visitor. It is 9 miles (15km) from Bridgetown (☎ 428-4803).

There are side roads off to the right which lead to the coast, especially at **Pilgrim Place**, where the road runs down to Chancery Lane, a spectacular area of cliffs and swamps. It is not always possible to drive all the way down to the beach, and you often have to find a safe place to park by the road and walk the final stretch.

Continue past the airport keeping to the secondary roads which run closer to the coastline. Again, there are small side roads leading to the coast at **Salt Cave**, **Harmony Lodge** and **Ocean City**, but continue through **Mangrove**, and then turn right for **Foul Bay**, so named because the anchorage was disliked by sailors. Don't worry, the beach is lovely.

The road runs along this impressive stretch of coastline past **Cobbler's Rock** and **Crane Bay**. The Crane Beach Hotel sits on the cliffs looking out over a dazzling stretch of white and pink coral sand beach. The area gets its name because ships used to anchor under the cliffs and cargo would be loaded and unloaded by a crane on top of the cliff. The coral stone hotel was opened in 1867 and is the island's oldest. It is popular with honeymooners, and noted for its sea food and you can laze away a few hours over an elegant lunch or candlelit dinner, or enjoy after-

Belair Golf Course

You could work off your lunch, or build up an appetite for it at the Belair Golf Course. It is a 3 par, 9-hole course although it can be played as an 18-hole course. The course is made more difficult because of a number of lakes and the considerable distraction of the stunning coastal views. The club is open daily from 7am (☎ 423-4653).

Crane Beach

noon tea. The hotel has an admission fee for non-residents which is deducted from any bill for food or drink.

The road then continues past **Shark's Hole** to **Sam Lord's Castle**.

The magnificent Georgian fortified mansion was built in 1820, and is now part of the Marriotts resort, and has a sinister history, although much of it has been greatly embellished over the years.

Sam Lord's Castle

L egend has it that Samuel Hall Lord, a Barbadian planter, was also a wrecker, and that he made his fortune by tricking passing ships into sailing on to the reefs where they foundered and he could plunder them. He would place lanterns on the castle walls and surrounding cliffs to trick the ship's captain into thinking they must be the lights of Bridgetown. The ship would head for the lights and hit the reefs. It is said that treasures looted from the sinking ships were stored in the castle's dungeons. As befitting a larger than life character, when Sam Lord died, he left mountainous debts.

The building is still magnificent with splendid mahogany columns in the dining room, ornate plaster ceilings, and antique Bajan furnishings and paintings. The gardens with their fountains are also a delight. It is possible to stay in Sam Lord's room and sleep in what is reputed to be his large four poster bed.

There is a small admission charge.

Shark's Hole is a spectacular and photogenic area with impressive cliffs which obviously inspired the early settlers who named part of the coastline **Beachy Head**, presumably after the coastal chalk cliffs in the south of England.

Places to visit inland

Daphne's Sea Shell Studio

From Sam Lord's Castle, head inland to **Ruby**, past the **King George V Memorial Park** gardens, then take the secondary road which runs south and to the right of the park for Daphne's Sea Shell Studio on the Congo Road Plantation. It is just off highway 5 at Six Cross Roads. Look for the pink signs.

The studio is housed in the outbuildings, once used as a cowshed, of the elegant old great house that is famous for its unique coral stone archway and spectacular driveway. You can watch Daphne and other members of her family at work producing shell pictures, jewelry, picture frames and hand carved chattel houses. They also design and produce hand-painted cotton clothing. The studio is open from 9am to 5pm Monday to Friday, and from 9am to 4pm on Saturday (☎ 423-6180).

Foursquare Rum Factory and Heritage Park

South of Six Cross Roads is the Foursquare Rum Factory and Heritage Park. The distillery, on a former sugar plantation, is the newest and most modern in the region. There are tours of the distillery that is surrounded by a number of shops, galleries and eateries. There is also a small theme park, pet farm, children's play park and sugar machinery museum. There is also the **Cane Pit Amphitheatre** (☎ 420-1977).

Sunbury Plantation House

Then continue to the crossroads at Marchfield, and turn right for Sunbury Plantation House. This is one of the oldest and grandest of the island's Great Houses, and a listed building.

It tragically burnt down in July 1995, the week after an attempted break in, but it has been faithfully restored and is now open to the public. The house is over 300 years old and beautifully furnished as it would have been when the owners were in residence in the 18th and 19th centuries.

Of special interest were the unique collection of Barbados mahogany furniture, Georgian silver and original prints, all sadly lost. The fine collection of horse-drawn carriages under cover, and plantation vehicles such as ox carts, scattered around the lovely grounds were saved and can still be seen. The house was a haunt of Sam Lord who ate there regularly.

The grounds, courtyard and woodland are also open to the public and there is a snack bar and gift shop. You can also experience the 'Planter's Candelit Dinner', a five-course feast around the 200-year old table where Sam Lord was a regular guest. The house is open daily from 10am to 5pm and the last tour starts at 4.30pm (☎ 423-6270).

Coral Stone Quarry & St Philip Parish Church

A little to the west of Sunbury Plantation in **Ebenezer** is the Coral

Stone Quarry. It has provided much of the coral stone used in Bridgetown over the last 100 years. A little north along highway 4B is St Philip Parish Church, the fifth church on the site since 1649. The church was destroyed by fire in 1977 but has been fully restored.

Bushy Park Race Circuit

After leaving the plantation turn right for **Padmore** and Bushy Park Race Circuit. It is also the home of **Karting Barbados** with its international racetrack and Track Side Bar. It is open from 9am to 5.30pm Monday to Saturday (☎ 423-7789).

Oughterson Plantation, Barbados Zoo & the Wildlife Park

Then head north a short distance for the Oughterson Plantation, a former sugar plantation and mill and the home of the Barbados Zoo. You can visit the Great House where arts and crafts are on sale, and the **wildlife park**, which opened in 1983, with a collection of animals housed in the former outbuildings and paddocks.

There are several species of monkeys, agoutis, alligators, snakes and turtles, exotic birds as well as an education center and nature trail through the orchards. There is a special petting area for children. It specializes in promoting and conserving the island's flora and fauna. There is an admission charge. It is open from 9am to 5pm Monday to Saturday and from 10.15am to 5pm on Sunday (☎ 423-6203).

If you want to visit the above attractions as a separate day out, you continue this tour from Sam Lord's Castle by following the coastal secondary road north around the eastern bulge of the island past a number of bays and coves, all of which are worth visiting. **Bottom Bay** is delightful, completely surrounded by cliffs and with gently-swaying coconut palms for shade. There is even a small cave to explore.

From the wildlife park at Oughterson Plantation the route continues by driving north a short distance to connect with highway 4B. Turn right and then at **Thicket** turn left for **Bath** with one of the few 'safe' swimming beaches on the east coast.

The route continues past **Kitridge Bay** and the **East Point Lighthouse**, and then swings round to head west past **Ragged Point**, the most easterly point on Barbados. You can reach Rugged Point from the bumpy road that leads to the old lighthouse. The small detour is worthwhile because there are fabulous views right along the east coastline.

Retrace your route to the highway and then continue on past **Culpepper Island** – the island's only offshore possession – to **Skeete's Bay** and **Cummins Hole**. You then cut inland in a loop that takes you close to **Three Houses**, the site of one of the railway stations along the line that used to run from Bridgetown to Bathsheba and Belleplaine. You can also visit the ruins of a sugar mill, set in a park landscaped by the National Conservation Commission.

Follow the loop round to the coast and head north to Bath. The road then connects with the main tour at Thicket when you make a right turn for **Palmers**, a beautifully

(cont'd on page 84)

Long Bay

Daphne's Sea Shell Studio

Sunbury Plantation House

restored Plantation House with restaurant and attractive grounds. It is then a short drive to Codrington College.

Codrington College

The house and grounds are magnificent and reflect the lifestyle of the brilliant Christopher Codrington, who at the age of only thirty became Captain General and Governor of the Leeward Islands. He died in 1710 and in his will ordained that the estate become a theological college.

The seminary buildings date from 1743 and the college opened in 1745. It is the oldest existing seminary in the Western Hemisphere. From 1875 to 1955 the college was associated with the University of Durham, but since then has been affiliated with the University of the West Indies, and is the theological college for the Anglican Church in the Province of the West Indies, and a conference center.

Because it is in use there is limited access to the buildings but the grounds can be visited. There is an interpretive nature trail through the gardens that contain many of the plants found on the island, and there is a wonderful huge lily pond, manicured lawns and appropriately named royal palms, also known as cabbage palms. According to legend, Princes Albert and George who visited the estate in 1879, each planted a palm. The palm planted by Prince Albert withered and died, and shortly afterwards news arrived from England that the prince had also died.

The route then continues to Bath past **Conset Bay**. This is a beauti-ful sheltered bay and most afternoons you can see the fishermen come ashore with their catch.

Continue to **Newcastle** and **Martin's Bay**, and the route then heads south to visit St John's Church.

St John's Church

The first church was built in the 1660s but destroyed by the Great Hurricane of 1831, and the present Gothic structure was consecrated in 1836. The church, on a hill at 800 feet (244m) above sea level, has magnificent views over the east coast, and the cemetery contains the grave of Ferdinand Paleologus, a direct descendant of Constantine the Great, the last Byzantine Emperor, who was dethroned when the Turks captured Constantinople in the 15th century.

Ferdinand came to Barbados as a refugee and was a church warden from 1655 and vestryman until his death on 3 October 1678. He was buried in the churchyard and his tomb was unearthed during the 1831 hurricane with his head pointing to the west according to Greek Orthodox custom. He was re-interred in the inscribed vault that can be seen today. The pulpit is of special interest as it is built from six different island woods – mahogany, ebony, locust, machineel, oak and pine.

Snacks and souvenirs are available from the shop that is run in aid of the church funds.

Pat's Arts and Crafts is a short distance from the church and is a small country shop selling locally made goods at prices well below those often found in Bridgetown and other tourist areas. There is local pottery, hand-made jewelry, wire craft and straw work (☎ 433-1287).

Also on highway 3B closer to **Gun Hill**, is **Orchid World** that has thousands of plants on display. It is open daily from 9am to 5pm (☎ 433-0306).

At Four Cross Roads, turn to visit Villa Nova, another magnificent example of a sugar plantation Great House. It is set on the hillside at 840 feet (256m) above sea level and commands wonderful views over the lush St John Valley. The house was built in 1834 by Edmund Haynes, a sugar baron, and set in magnificent landscaped and ornamental gardens.

Villa Nova

The Earl of Avon, formerly Sir Anthony Eden and British Prime Minister at the time of the Suez Crisis, bought the property from the Barbados Government in the 1960s and in 1966 hosted a visit by Queen Elizabeth II and Prince Philip. The Queen commemorated the visit by planting two portlandias, famous for their fragrant flowers, which can still be seen. The house, which has changed little since it was first built, is set to become Barbados' first Country House Hotel with three gourmet restaurants (☎ 433-1524).

The Cotton Tower

North of Villa Nova is the Cotton Tower, one of a string of military signal towers that crossed the island. It is named after Lady Caroline Cotton, daughter of Lord Combermere, the Governor of Barbados. She laid the foundation stone in 1819. The tower has been well restored by the Barbados National Trust.

Return to highway 3B, and if you want to make a short detour, cross over and continue until you reach highway 4 and turn right for a short distance to view Drax Hall. The house is not open to the public and has been owned by the same family since it was built around the middle of the 17th century.

Drax Hall

The hall is interesting for two reasons, it was the first place on Barbados that sugar cane was planted in the late-1640s and it vies with Nicholas Abbey as the oldest building on the island.

The 878-acre (351-hectare) estate is believed to be the only one in the West Indies to have been owned by the same family throughout its life. The Great House, built by brothers James and William Drax, is a good example of Jacobean architecture, and has a fine wooden Jacobean staircase. William was a remarkable man. He not only made a fortune by planting sugar, but he managed to be knighted by Cromwell and was created a baronet four years later by Charles II.

Francia Plantation

Head back to highway 3B and turn left and continue towards Bridgetown to visit the well signposted Francia Plantation. The house was built at the beginning of the 20th century by a wealthy Brazilian farmer of French descent, who married a Barbadian woman. It is still owned and occupied by their descendents, and is a working plantation producing tropical crops.

It is on a wooded hill and looks out over the St George Valley.

The beautiful building combines both their origins with European and Caribbean architectural styles and Brazilian wood paneling. There is an impressive flight of stone steps up to the triple arched front entrance, and the white painted walls contrast attractively with the red roofs, and the lush green vegetation of the creepers and ferns draping the verandah and walls.

It has a magnificent collection of antique Barbadian furniture, an unusual chandelier with its own hurricane shades, and a priceless 1522 map of the West Indies. There are also many paintings of the area, including several watercolors of the Gun Hill signal station painted by Lionel Grimstone Fawkes in the late 1870s.

St John's Church

The terraced gardens are also a delight with their fountains, ferneries and lawns. The house is open Monday to Friday from 10am to 4pm. There is an admission charge (☎ 429-0474).

Gun Hill Signal Station

Further south off highway 3B is the Gun Hill Signal Station, built on top of the cliffs by the British in 1818, as one of a chain used to warn of the approach of enemy ships, and flash the information around the island. It stands at 700 feet (213m) above sea level, and has commanding views over the southern half of the island.

The hill's strategic importance was recognized very early on and two cannon were stationed on the crest. At that time it was known as Briggs Hills but the name changed when the cannon were installed. The cannon were not designed to fire at an enemy, but to be fired to alert the garrison of any imminent threat. When the signal station was built the quarters also included a small convalescent wing for military from the coastal garrison. Because of the altitude it was cooler than on the coast and a better place to recover from the many illnesses that afflicted the soldiers, especially malaria and yellow fever.

A late afternoon or early evening visit is the best time to appreciate the views. The signal station, which looks more like a small church from a distance, has been well restored by the National Trust, and is reached along a one-way track.

It now houses a small museum and one of the many interesting exhibits is a magnificent white rampant lion carved from a huge boulder on the hillside just below the signal station by Henry Wilkinson, a British officer in 1868, who presumably didn't have too much else to do. The road runs below the lion but there is a path up to it. It is open from 9am to 4pm Monday to Saturday. There is a small admission charge (☎ 429-1358).

St George Parish Church

Drive past Rowans Rectory to St George Parish Church, one of the oldest on the island. Built in 1784 it was one of only four parish churches on Barbados to survive the hurricane of 1831. Its most important feature is the 18th century altar painting entitled *The Resurrection* by Benjamin West, who was the first American President of the Royal Academy. The painting is also of note because of the centurion's black patch.

After the artist's death, the picture was in store at Lower Estate when a thief broke in. The thief claimed that the centurion's eye watched him as he searched the room, so he poked it out. Covering the damaged area with the patch restored the painting. It was later donated to the church by Henry Frere.

Among the sculptures there is one by Richard Westmacott whose most famous work is the statue of Nelson in Trafalgar Square, Bridgetown.

Government House

Keep on to the Charles Rowe Bridge then south to connect with highway 4 that runs back into the capital. At **Mangera** you can turn left to visit Government House.

It was originally called Pilgrim House and was purchased by the Government from John Pilgrim, a Quaker in 1736, to act as the official residence of the Governor of Barbados. It is very sturdily built with thick walls which is why it has managed to survive so many hurricanes, and combines most of the features of a traditional Great House with full-length shady verandahs, arched porticos, parapet roof and impressive sweeping driveway.

Also typical of the Caribbean are the jalousie louvered shutters. The shutters can be closed when a storm is blowing, and the louvered slats can be opened or closed to control the amount of light and air. Jalousie comes from the French word for jealousy, presumably because when adjusted properly, one could look out and see what was going on without being seen. The gardens on the east front are said to have been the inspiration for those at Villa Nova.

Ilaro Court & Errol Barrow Memorial Park

A short drive to the west of Government House is Ilaro Court, designed in 1919 by Lady Gilbert Carter, the American wife of Sir Gilbert Carter, who was Governor of Barbados from 1904 to 1911.

The large house built in coral stone, stands in superbly landscaped gardens with many beautiful trees, including mahogany. It is a slightly strange mix of architectural styles, combining carved Ionic columns and features from traditional Great Houses. The house was bought by the Government in 1976 and completely restored as the official residence of the Prime Minister.

Also nearby is the Errol Barrow Memorial Park, opened in November 1987, in memory of the former premier before Independence and long serving Prime Minister following it. He died in office in 1987.

Emancipation Monument

To the east of Government House on highway 5 at the crossroads near the Sherbourne Centre is the Emancipation Monument. It is the statue of a slave whose chains have been broken, and whose arms are raised to the sky. The statue is affectionately known as Bussa by many islanders, after the slave on Bayley's Plantation who led the 1816 uprising, the largest in the island's history. The statue, the work of leading Barbadian sculptor Karl Broodhagen, was erected in 1985.

THE NORTHERN TOUR

The route takes highway 2 north from Bridgetown past the Bush Hall National Stadium and the historic Tyrol Cot Heritage Village.

Bathsheba

Tyrol Cot Heritage Village

The house was built of coral stone blocks and bricks brought across as ship's ballast, in the mid-19th century by William Farnum, a prominent builder, and from 1929 was the home of Sir Grantley Adams, one of the island's leading statesmen. He founded the Barbados Labour Party, was the first Premier of Barbados and the only Prime Minister of the ill-fated West Indies Federation. His son J M 'Tom' Adams, was also born there, and he was Prime Minister from 1976 until his death in office in 1985.

The house, restored by the National Trust, features antique Bajan mahogany furniture while the grounds contain a reconstructed chattel house and craft village. Each house displays the work of a traditional craftsman working on site. There is also a working blacksmiths and you can eat at the Old Stables Restaurant. It is open from Monday to Friday 9am to 5pm (☎ 424-2074).

Cross over the ABC National Highway, which is named after three of the country's most eminent statesmen who served as either premier before Independence or Prime Minister after 1966. They were Mr Tom Adams 1976-85, Mr Errol Barrow 1961-76 and 1986-7 and Mr Gordon Cummins 1958-61. It provides a fast link between the International airport and the west coast resorts.

Shortly after, you reach the **Sharon Maravian Church** on the left. The Moravians were the first missionaries with a declared vocation to educate the slaves and convert them to Christianity. They arrived in Barbados in 1765 and the church was built at Sharon in 1799. It was destroyed in the 1831 hurricane but rebuilt as before so is one of the few buildings that

truly reflect 18th century architecture without any additions or alterations. It is noted for its tower and windows.

Follow the signposts to **Edgehill** and the Future Centre and the Earthworks Pottery and Gallery. The **Future Centre** is an interactive model for sustainable living which stresses organic farming and recycling. Visit the aptly named **Tire Garden** and dine on the freshest of organic vegetables in the Fronds Restaurant (☎ 425-2020).

Then proceed to the **Earthworks Pottery** where you can watch Goldie Spieler and her son David, together with their team of potters making and decorating their very individual Barbadian earthenware which ranges from the functional to the exotic. **The Potters House Gallery** is next door and offers a

Future Centre

range of arts and crafts such as woodcarvings, island jewelry, batik and other hand-painted fabrics. It is open from 9am to 5pm Monday to Friday and from 9am to 1pm on Saturday (☎ 425-0223).

Welchman Hall Gully is another marvelous National Trust property and offers a delightful walk along a trail through a deep gully packed with exotic plants and trees and hanging vines. More than 200 species of plants, including clove, banana, fig and nutmeg can be seen along the trail which is along the floor of a massive ancient cave. Permeating ground water and underground streams are thought to have carved out these massive caves through the soft limestone. Harder surrounding rocks resisted erosion and account for the steep sides. At some point the roof collapsed transforming the cave into a gully. There are also a number of interesting coral rock formations.

From about 1860 the owners of the property started the planting program introducing tropical plants from around the world. Sadly, the estate became neglected and by the time the National Trust acquired the property in 1962 it had become overgrown.

Today, the trails wander through marvelous stands of mature trees, giant groves of bamboo and a dazzling array of tropical plants and flowers. Because of the steep cliffs and overhead canopy of leaves, the gully is usually very cool, an added bonus if you want to escape from the heat of the day. You can also spot monkeys. The property is open daily from 9am to 5pm (☎ 438-6671).

Harrison's Cave

It is well worth making the short detour to Harrison's Cave, by far the most magnificent subterranean attraction on the island. As surface water seeped through the limestone rock over millions of years, it carved out this magnificent series of caverns packed with underground streams and waterfalls, stalagmites and stalactites. Stalacmites grow up from the floor and stalactites hang from the ceiling (you can remember which is which, because stalactites have to hang on 'tight' to stop falling down). The cave was part of the same subterranean system that included Welchman Hall Gully.

There are many other examples of crystallized limestone formations. Swede Ollie Sorensen explored the caves and the National Trust then recommended that the Government open them to the public. The conducted tours through the illuminated caves are aboard electric trams. They can be visited daily between 9am and 4pm when the last tour leaves. There is an admission price and reservations are recommended (☎ 438-6640).

Highland Outdoor Tours, Cane Field, are based close to **Mount Misery**, one of the highest points on the island and the location offers spectacular views of both the Atlantic and Caribbean and everything between. You can take a trip in a tractor-drawn jitney, go for a horse ride or take a guided hike through land only recently opened up to the public (☎ 438-8069).

Bamboo Village

Return to highway 2 and head north to Bamboo Village. A few years ago, this was a gentle drive through unspoiled countryside. Then an islander noticed that tourists kept stopping to take pictures of the Atlantic coast from the bridge. She started to offer souvenirs, others joined her and now there is such a collection of stalls that it has become almost a compulsory stop for cruise ship and coach tours. The village gets its name because the locals started to build a bamboo hut and like Topsy, it has just kept on growing. Stop awhile to look at the wares and take some pictures.

The **Flower Forest of Barbados** is a lovely idea and another indication of how seriously conservation is being taken on the island. The 50-acre (20-hectare) forest is on the Old Richmond Plantation, close to Harrison's Cave and Welchman Hall Gully.

The forest is the brainchild of a group of individuals who wanted to preserve an area of tropical beauty, not just for their own pleasure but for future generations. The gardens contain a wide range of tropical fruit trees, exotic plants and flowers, and have been arranged so that apart from the immediate scenery, there are also wonderful views over palm groves and along the east coast. The area is also rich in wildlife with monkeys, mongoose and tropical birds.

A guided map helps you find your way through the forest and identifies many of the plants seen along the way. There are benches and an administration-information center, built around the original house sugar boiling where the sugar was boiled. Refreshments are available. It is open daily from 9am to 5pm (☎ 433-8152). There is an admission charge.

From the Flower Forest there are views of **Mount Hillaby** to the west, and almost equal distance between the Caribbean and Atlantic coasts. The mountain at 1,115 feet (343m) is the island's highest point. There is a narrow winding road close to the summit from the village of **Hillaby**, and the ascent is worthwhile for the views offered from the top.

Take the secondary road on right past Haggats for **Bathsheba**, a charming sleepy little village which is worth a visit, especially if you enjoy surfing. It has a beautiful setting with wonderful scenery inland, and the crashing waves rolling on from the Atlantic foaming as they swirl among the gigantic rocks in the water. Just offshore is the **Soup Bowl**, named because of

its foaming surf, which is the venue for both local and international surfing events.

The 20-room **Edgewater Inn** makes a great lunch stop and you can sit and watch the surfers from the cliffside bar and restaurant (☎ 433-9900). The inn was a private home at the beginning of the 20th century, and is now noted for its beautiful handmade mahogany furniture, leaded glass windows and ornate lamps – and its food.

It is worth noting that the beaches off St Andrew and St Joseph do have powerful waves and there may be riptides and undercurrents, so swimmers need to exercise caution. It is not suitable for young children or weak swimmers. **Cattle Wash Beach** is the longest beach on the island.

Top: The Flower Forest
Above: The east coast from near Boscobel

Andromeda Botanic Gardens

Also in Bathsheba, and overlooking the Atlantic are the Andromeda Botanic Gardens created by Iris Bannochie in 1954 and bequeathed by her in 1988 to the National Trust. It has been described as the "loveliest, most interesting and varied botanic garden in the Caribbean", and has been a regular winner at the prestigious UK Chelsea Flower Shower.

You can wander through brilliantly colorful and fragrant displays of hibiscus, bougainvillea, heliconia and orchids. There are lily ponds, waterfalls and streams running through the gardens to the ocean, and thousands of plants from around the tropical world, including many rare species. The plants form a series of collections separated by streams, ponds and rock outcrops.

There is a café and Best of Barbados shop. The 5 acre (2-hectare) gardens are open daily from 9am to 5pm (☎ 433-9261). Close to the botanic gardens is the **Bonito Bar and Restaurant** which is open from breakfast to late lunch, and is especially noted for its home cooked Bajan specialties and great Bajan Sunday brunch buffet (☎ 433-9034).

It gets its name because herds of cattle would be driven down from the hills into the sea for their annual bath. Today its rugged charm makes it a great place for a picnic or ramble but only venture into the sea if the lifeguard says it is safe.

It is worth making the short detour inland from Bathsheba on highway 3 past the **St Joseph Parish Church**, built in 1839 2 miles (3km) uphill from the site of the original church which was consecrated in 1641.

The turn left for **Buckden House** and **Easy Hall** follows the road east of the Malvern Plantation to visit **Hackleton's Cliff**, 1,000 feet (305m) above sea level and offering stunning views along the east coast. The view is at its best during the morning. This is the most impressive of several inland cliffs on Barbados, which used to represent the coastline before further upheaval took place and the island rose further out of the sea. According to legend, the cliff is named after a man called Hackleton who, having lost his fortune, rode his horse at full gallop over the edge. Great care needs to be taken close to the edge of cliff.

After experiencing the view, visit **Joe's River Tropical Rain Forest**, which lies between Hackleton's Cliff and the Atlantic. It is an 85-acre (34-hectare) area of woodlands. Start at Hackleton's Cliff and follow the trail which descends into the woods which have a wide range of trees. The area is run by the National Conservation Commission which has created trails and picnic areas, and there are wood cabins, for those who want to spend longer communing with nature (☎ 425-1200).

Just south of St Joseph Parish Church there is a side road to the Cotton Tower, another of the signaling stations spanning the island. It has been restored by the National Trust and can be viewed daily.

Return to the coast and turn left on to the scenic **East Coast Road**, which was opened by Queen Elizabeth II in 1966. There is a commemorative plaque on a huge boulder at the northern end of the road. The road follows the line of an old railroad and the remains of some of the stations can still be seen along the way.

Barclay's Park is a 50-acre (20-hectare) recreation park, north of Bathsheba on the east coast, which was presented to the Government and people of Barbados by Barclay's Bank in 1966 to commemorate the island's independence. There is a snack bar and changing rooms, but because of the waves, it is not really suitable for weak swimmers. There are also some very interesting rum shops in this area.

The Chalky Mount Potteries

It is worth making the short scenic detour inland from the park to Chalky Hill to visit The Chalky Mount Potteries. From a distance, the hill resembles a resting man with his hands folded on his stomach. Locals refer to this geological gentleman as Napoleon. The village is known for its potters who have been producing their wares from local clay for more than 300 years. Many of them use the traditional potters wheel which has not changed for hundreds of years. You can watch the craftsmen at work for a small fee, and buy their wares. Two special pots made here are the canarees, used for serving soups and stews, and monkeys that are jugs, used for storing water. They are still made to their traditional design that has not changed for at least 400 years.

The East Coast Road then runs inland beyond **Windy Hill** to connect with highway 2 near the police station. Just south of the junction is a minor road that runs into the hills through **Belle Hill** to **Turner's Hall Woods** and **Turner's Hall** at the end of the road, close to Mount Hillaby. The woods contain many species of trees, including silk cotton, sandbox, trumpet tree, locust, cabbage palm and the macaw palm. A visit to the woods is interesting because it gives you an idea of what the whole island must have been like when the first settlers arrived to find Barbados covered completely in tropical forest.

Continue past **Walkers Savannah** and **Long Pond** to **St Andrew Parish Church**. Follow highway 2 to visit **Farley Hill** and the **Barbados Wildlife Reserve** (see below) that is across the road. Farley Hill was the site of the island's grandest 19th century Great House. It was destroyed by fire in the late 1950s and the gov-ernment bought the surrounding 17 acres (7 hectares) of parkland in 1965 to create the Farley Hill National Park. It is worth a visit for the stunning ocean views.

Almost next door to the Wildlife Reserve is the **Grenade Hall Forest and Signal Station** that is another good example of how eco-tourism can work – the preservation and conservation of history and natural history while still providing a tourist attraction. There is a 3-mile (5km) interpretive walk along coral stone paths, through the forest to the restored 19th century signaling tower which has tremendous views, and allows you to see how messages could rapidly be flashed around the island to warn of impending danger.

During the restoration, more than 6,000 artifacts, including pre-Columbian tools, were found, and many of these are on display. Along the path there are signs explaining how the various trees, shrubs and

Barbados Wildlife Reserve

The reserve endeavors to show animals in their natural surroundings and as unrestricted as possible. It was established in 1985 in 4 acres (1.6 hectares) of natural mahogany forest. All the buildings are made from coral stone gathered from the surrounding sugar cane fields, and the pathway bricks come from 17th and 18th century sugar mills.

It also offers the chance to interact with many of the animals. You can monkey about with the Barbados green monkeys in the forest, and see iguana, a colony of rare red-footed tortoises, endangered hare, mongoose, small muntjac brocket deer, agoutis, armadillos and many other animals and birds in the exotic surroundings. Imported species include otter, wallaby and South American alligators. There is also a walk-through aviary, breeding area, nature trail and information and education center. Refreshments are available. It is open daily from 10am to 5pm. Monkey feeding is at 4pm. There is an admission charge (☎ 422-8826).

herbs were used for medicinal, culinary and other uses (☎ 422-8826).

Farley Hill National Park, opposite the Barbados Wildlife Reserve, is a beautiful, peaceful area where you can walk among the shady trees and admire the flowers and wildlife. The park is part of an old sugar plantation and the remains of the old Great House, destroyed by fire in the 1960s, can be seen. From the mid-19th century, the Great House was owned by Sir Graham Briggs. His reputation for lavish hospitality was legendary.

You might also see a monkey or two in the trees. The park is open daily from 7am to 6pm (☎ 422-8724).

Continue to **Portland Plantation**, and then take the secondary road on the right to visit the strangely named **Cherry Tree Hill**. In fact, the road actually runs through an avenue of beautiful old mahogany trees to a viewpoint at 850 feet (259m) above sea level, overlooking the rugged Scotland District and Cattle Wash Beach. The road then runs steeply downhill to the **Morgan Lewis Mill**.

Morgan Lewis Mill

The mill is the only windmill on the island, and believed to be the only one in the Caribbean, with its wheelhouse and sails in working order. As a result, it is now among the World Monuments Fund list of 100 Most Endangered Sites in the World. The windmill is similar to those found in Holland, because mills like this were introduced to Barbados by the Dutch Jews who moved to the island from Brazil and were responsible for introducing sugar cane and the processes for making molasses and rum.

At one time, there were more than 500 windmills on the island, and while a few remain, none is so complete. In fact, the mill, which was operational until 1947, is believed to be the best preserved in the Caribbean. The mill, which contains a small museum and exhibition center, is maintained by the National Trust, and is open daily from 9am to 5pm. There is a small admission charge (☎ 422-9222).

St Nicholas Abbey

From Morgan Lewis Mill you should take in the small detour to visit St Nicholas Abbey. If you needed further proof of just how wealthy Barbados must have been during the days when King Sugar reigned supreme, you have only to visit this magnificent Jacobean-style stone Great House, believed to be the oldest in Barbados. It is not known why it was called the Abbey, but it is one of only three Jacobean houses remaining in the Western Hemisphere.

It was designed by an English architect unfamiliar with Barbados weather and this explains why there are so many fireplaces! It was built around 1650 for Colonel Benjamin Berringer. He considered that his neighbor John Yeamans was paying too much attention to his wife and challenged the man to a duel. Unfortunately, he was killed, so John (later Sir) Yeamans, married Mrs Berringer and became the owner of the Abbey. A court later returned the estate to Berringer's children. In 1663, Yeamans set out from Speightstown to establish a colony in the Carolinas and later became Governor of South Carolina. The house is full of wonderful antique English and Bajan furniture and furnishings, including a full 1810 Coalport dinner service, and early Wedgwood portrait miniatures.

Of especial interest is a black and white home movie shot in 1935 showing Speightstown and other island scenes. The film is shown twice daily at 11am and 2pm. The house is open from Monday to Friday 10am to 3pm (☎ 422-8725).

If you cut inland a little further from St Nicholas Abbey you can visit the **Castle Pottery**. The pottery is a five-minute drive from the abbey and you can watch the skilled craftsman either creating the pottery by hand or shaping it on wheels. It is open daily from 10am to 4.30pm.

Then head for the coast and follow the secondary road that runs parallel with the north-east coast to Gay's Cove, Pico Tenerife and Paul's Point. **Pico Tenerife** is a 269 feet (82m) high pinnacle of rock off **Gay's Cove**.

This stretch of coastline to the northern tip of the island at **North Point** is very spectacular with its cliffs. There are only a handful of minor roads offering access to the beach with the final part of the journey having to be made on foot, to the appropriately named **Ladder Bay** for instance. It is worth making the trip to **River Bay**, so called because a number of streams run into the bay at this point. It is a good place to picnic and explore but while you can wade in the streams, don't go into the bay where there are very strong undercurrents.

Keep on the secondary roads which run parallel with the north western coastline past Cluffs Bay, the beautiful and popular Archers Bay, Stroud Bay and Norse's Bay to **Harrison Point Lighthouse**, one of three lighthouses on the island still operating.

It is worth detouring inland to visit the **St Lucy Parish Church** and the **Mount Gay Distillery** at Fairmount.

The distillery is named after the hill that overlooks Gay's Cove. The distillery has been producing world class rum since the 1800s and now produces around 500,000 gallons (2,250,000 litres) of spirits a day. The rum is shipped in barrels to Bridgetown where it is blended and bottled. The distillery can be visited daily between 8am and 4pm and there are great views along the coast from its hilltop position.

Animal Flower Cave

Close to North Point is the Animal Flower Cave, a delightful place on the northernmost tip of the island. The cave is really a series of small caverns, carved out by the sea over tens of thousands of years, and gets its name because it was home to large numbers of multi-colored sea anemones, whose swaying tentacles resemble flowers. The number of anemones, however, has declined sharply in recent years.

The waves have also carved the rocks into strange shapes, and with a little imagination you can make out stone frogs and lizards. The cave floor was carved out about 500,000 years ago, and at the turn of the last century was a popular venue for dances. The steps down were originally carved to accommodate the dancers.

It is normally open daily from 9am to 5pm but may be closed if the seas are too rough, so check first (☎ 439-8797). There is a bar and restaurant and an admission charge.

The Georgian parish church, near the Sir Theodore Brancker roundabout, dates from 1837. The original wooden structure was built in 1627 and replaced with a stone building in 1741.

The rugged area inland is known as the **Scotland District**, and gets its name because it resembles parts of the Scottish highlands. Many of the Anglo Catholics 'Barbadosed' by Cromwell were settled here.

Take highway 1C back to the coast and connect with highway 1B for **Speightstown**, once known as Little Bristol because it was such a busy port, and many of the trading ships came from Bristol. Much of the island's sugar was shipped from the port and because this was such a valuable commodity Speightstown was protected by a ring of forts. Some of the cannon can still be seen along the Esplanade.

Arbib Nature and Heritage Trail

It is worth exploring the award-winning Arbib Nature and Heritage Trail. It offers an insight into the natural history and heritage of Speightstown and the Whim Gully, In fact, there are two trails, a 4.7-mile (7.5 km) hike which traverses the Whim Gully and Warleigh, one of the last working plantations, to the 18th century **Dover fort**. There is also a less demanding 3.4 mile (5.5 km) trail. Trail guides can be booked through the tourist office (☎ 426-2421).

The town was named after planter and Bristol merchant William Speight, a member of the first Barbados Parliament in 1639. **St Peter's Church** was destroyed in the 1830 hurricane, rebuilt in Georgian style in 1837 and largely destroyed by fire in 1980. It was rebuilt and re-consecrated in 1983. The town has many fine old wooden buildings with their overhanging balconies, and a good selection of Bajan restaurants.

Further north, **Port St Charles** is nearing completion. This development combines exclusive million-dollar homes and full marina facilities. It will eventually become the island's main port of entry after Bridgetown.

Down the coast there is a bay known as **Six Men's Bay** that is said to have got its name because the English settlers found six Indians there. While there is no evidence of an Indian settlement at this time, Indian artifacts have been found in caves inland, especially around Mount Brevitor. It is still an important boat building center.

The area back along the coast into Bridgetown contains many luxury hotels, resorts and expensive villas. There are wonderful beaches and lots of restaurants and rum shops which earned it the name 'The Gold Coast', and more recently, as more tourist dollars have flowed in, it has been upgraded to 'The Platinum Coast'.

Continue south to **Mullins Bay** one of the west coast's most popular beaches and home of The Legend Restaurant, which is consistently voted one of the best on the island. Reservations are recommended (☎ 422-0631).

North Point

Sir Frank Hutson Sugar Machinery Museum

Holetown Monument

Below left: St Lucy Parish Church
Below right: Grenade Hall Station

Mullins Beach Bar and Restaurant is a fun all-day place, with good Bajan food, a very late night bar and interesting murals.

Tony's Riding School at Gibbs Hill offers country, picnic and beach escorted rides and there are horses and ponies to suit all ages and levels of expertise. Hard hats are supplied (☎ 422-1549).

The **Shell Gallery**, similar to the one in Hastings, also has a tremendous shell collection and hand made shell jewelry and works of art.

At **Folkstone** you can visit the **Underwater Park and Museum**. This is a shallow water area suitable for most snorkelers and there is a marked underwater trail that can be followed through the inshore Dottins Reef. An aquarium and interpretive center has exhibits about the reef and its flora and fauna. It is next to St James Parish Church and is open from 10am to 5pm Sunday to Friday. There is a small admission charge, a playground for children, boat hire and rest rooms (☎ 422-2871).

St James Parish Church is on the outskirts of Holetown (see opposite). It is one of the four oldest on the island and close to the site of the first settlement on Barbados. It is claimed that parts of the lower levels of the church walls are the original structure but this has not been proved. It is known that the south entrance and porch tower, is at least 300 years old, and the font is inscribed 1684. The church bell is inscribed 'God Bless King William, 1696'. In 1982 President Ronald Reagan, the first US President to visit Barbados, attended church services here with his wife Nancy.

At **Sandy Lane Bay** there is the 18-hole championship Sandy Lane Golf Course. The Sandy Lane Hotel, built by Ronald Tree, played a major role in establishing Barbados as the holiday playground of the rich and famous, and guests have included Princess Margaret and Jacqueline Kennedy Onassis, Sir David Niven and Mick Jagger. To the south is **Holder's House**, an-

Sir Frank Hutson Sugar Machinery Museum

At **Portvale** you can visit the modern sugar factory and the Sir Frank Hutson Sugar Machinery Museum, the only sugar museum on the island. You can compare the modern hi-tech factory which was modernized in 1982, with the old boiling house that has been re-created in the grounds. The boiling house was already in existence when the steam engine was installed in 1882.

The factory produces about 1,500 tonnes of sugar a week during the harvest, and a by-product of the production process is the generation of 800 kilowatts of electricity which is fed into the national grid. The museum traces the history of sugar cane on the island from the 1640s and explains how it is grown and processed, it also displays the old equipment and machinery used in the plantations and sugar mills. It is open Monday to Saturday from 9am to 5pm (☎ 432-0100).

Holetown

Holetown was founded in 1627 as Jamestown when the first settlers led by Captain John Powell landed from the sailing ship *Olive Blossom* on 14 May. It is said that the ship's crew thought the area was similar to Limehouse Hole, a stretch of water on the River Thames in London's docklands, and so they called it Holetown, the name by which it later became known.

The **Holetown Monument** marks their landing and is the scene of an annual celebration. The monument is said to stand on the site of a fustic tree on which Captain Powell carved the name of King James, after declaring the island an English possession.

The town was originally called Jamestown, but Captain Powell did not realize that when he carved the King's name, James had already died. The remains of Fort James are behind the police station that is housed in the former gunners quarters still guarded by cannon.

There are a number of shops and eating places along 1st and 2nd Streets. The town's major event is the Holetown Festival that is held every February. Originally it celebrated the anniversary of the founding of the first settlement and it still starts at the Holetown Monument. Today, however, it is a celebration of local crafts and music with street parades, shows and entertainment.

other old Great House with very thick walls, which once stood in the middle of a 500-acre (200-hectare) sugar and tobacco plantation.

Inland from Sandy Lane and just off highway 2a is the **Bagatelle Great House**, now one of the island's top restaurants. The house was built by Lord Willoughby in 1645 and was the official residence of the Governor. It was originally called Parkham Park House but the name changed in 1877. According to local stories, the owner lost the house after a heavy gambling session but did not seem very concerned, saying it was just a 'bagatelle'. It became a restaurant in 1970. It is set in beautiful tropical gardens that are floodlit at night, and there is a small museum about the house's history.

Close to **Batts Rock Bay** is a house with high walls which was the island's leper colony. It was later used as the island's first radio station.

The modern campus of the **University of the West Indies** is on **Cave Hill** and overlooks Bridgetown and the port. The campus was opened in 1963 and has faculties of law, education, social services, natural sciences, arts and general studies. Part of the medical faculty is located at the Queen Elizabeth Hospital in Bridgetown. Cricket legend Sir Frank Worrell, is buried on the campus.

Also just outside the city limits are the **Lazaretto Gardens**, a haven of tranquility. The beautifully landscaped gardens have a magnificent waterfall, and are also home of the Barbados National Archives.

West India Rum Refinery

It is the oldest distillery in the world, and produces 500, 000 gallons of the spirit every year. There is a very interesting guided tour that lasts between 30-40 minutes, and includes a brief video presentation and the chance to visit the aging cellars, blending room and bottling plant. The tour ends with a tasting of Mount Gay rums, served on the verandah of a traditional Bajan house overlooking the sea. There is a souvenir shop and the chance to buy your preferred rum. The distillery is open from 9am to 5pm Monday to Friday and from 10am to 1pm on Saturday (☎ 425-8757).

The West India Rum Refinery, on Spring Garden Highway, is home of the **Cockspur Rum** and **Malibu**, both of which are exported around the world. The seafront visitors center offers Wednesday lunch tours which include a tour of the distillery, Bajan buffet to the sounds of a steel band, and copious amounts of rum. Free transportation is also provided (☎ 425-9393).

The **Mount Gay Visitor Centre**, also on Spring Garden Highway on the western outskirts of Bridgetown, has a tour of the distillery plus bar and souvenir shop.

You pass the **Kensington Oval**, home of cricket test matches in Barbados, as you drive back into Bridgetown. The grounds have been the home of cricket since 1892 when the owner of the Kensington Estate, Mr Foster Alleyne, rented the ground to the Pickwick Club for a nominal rent of one penny a year. In 1895 the first international was played when the island eleven played the visiting English team.

Note: New restaurants are opening all the time, established ones close down and others change their name or location. As a result, this restaurant listing is meant as a guide, not as a definitive list. If you discover a new restaurant or one that we have overlooked, please let us know. Prices are represented as $ inexpensive, $$ moderate and $$$ expensive.

Bridgetown and the West Coast

Abdul's $-$$
Indian. *Bay Street, Bridgetown,*
☎ 437-7680

Amy's Place $$
West Indian-Bajan. *Broad Street, Bridgetown,*
☎ 429-7854

Angry Annie's $-$$
American-Bajan-seafood-pasta. *Holetown,*
☎ 432-2119

Bagatelle Great House $$-$$$
Fine dining. *St Thomas,*
☎ 421-6767

Baku Brasserie $$
Imaginative bistro fare, lively nightspot.
Holetown, ☎ 432-2258

Balcony Cafe $
Snacks and lunches. *Cave Shepherd, Broad Street, Bridgetown,* ☎ 431-2088

Bamboo Beach Bar and Restaurant $$-$$
Seafood-Bajan. *Paynes Bay,* ☎ 432-2731

Barbados Pizza House $
Pasta-sandwiches. *Broad Street, Bridgetown,*
☎ 431-0500

Barbecue Barn $$
Excellent barbecue, grills and salads. *Holetown,*
☎ 419-8652

Beach House $$
Local and International.
St Peter, ☎ 422-5338

Bird's Nest $-$$
Caribbean. *Bay Street, Bridgetown,* ☎ 426-2807

Boatyard $-$$
Mediterranean Bistro, Very lively. *Carlisle Bay,*
☎ 436-2622

Bombas $-$$
Rasta-Pasta. *Paynes Bay,*
☎ 432-0569

Bourbon Street $$
Creole, blues and jazz.
Prospect, ☎ 424-4557

Brig (The) $$
Local and International.
Sunset, ☎ 432-1103

Brown Sugar $$
Bajan specialties. *Aquatic Gap,* ☎ 436-7069

Café Sublime $-$$
Local dishes and snacks.
Shallow Draught, Spring Garden, ☎ 436-8968

Carambola Restaurant $$-$$$
Elegant, seafood-International. *Derricks, St James,* ☎ 432-0832

The Chattel $
Bajan home cooking.
Holetown, ☎ 432-5278

Chefette $
Fast food chain with 10 locations.

Christophene $$-$$$
Gourmet dining.
Westmoreland,
☎ 422-3913

The Cliff $$$
Seafood-International, incredible location and service. *St James,*
☎ 432-1922

Club House Restaurant $$-$$$
Fine dining, reservations required. *Royal Westmoreland, St James,*
☎ 422-4653

Coach House Restaurant and Pub $$
Caribbean, Bajan specialties and seafood.
Sandy Lane, Paynes Bay,
☎ 432-1163

Cobblers Cove Restaurant $-$$$
Fine Continental dining.
Cobblers Cove Hotel,
☎ 422-2291

Cocomos $$
Bistro. *Holetown,*
☎ 432-0134

Colony Club $$-$$$
Fine Bajan-International.
St James Beach,
☎ 422-2335

Coconut Creek Club $$
International-Bajan.
Derricks, ☎ 432-0803

Coral Reef Club $$-$$$
Excellent Bajan cuisine.
St James Beach,
☎ 422-2372

Crocodile Den $$
Local and International.
Paynes, ☎ 432-7625

Discovery Bay $$
Bajan-International.
Holetown, ☎ 432-1301

Eating out on Barbados

**Drifters
Beach Bar
and Restaurant $$**
Crystal Cove,
☎ 432-2683

Emerald Palm $$
Bajan-International.
Porters, St James,
☎ 422-4116

Fathoms $$
Seafood. Paynes Bay,
☎ 432-2568

Fiesta $$
Prospect, St James,
☎ 425-1107

Fisherman's Pub $-$$
Bajan specialties and
entertainment.
Speightstown,
☎ 422-2703

**Fisherman's Wharf Bar
and Seafood Restaurant**
Seafood-Cajan.
Carenage, Bridgetown,
☎ 436-7778

Flamingo $$
International. Tamarind
Cove, ☎ 432-1332

Fountain Restaurant $$
Seafood-Bajan. Barbados
Beach Village,
☎ 425-1440

Garden Grill $$
Good value Bajan-
International cooking.
Holetown, ☎ 432-7711

Garden Restaurant $$
Bajan. Discovery Bay,
Holetown, ☎ 432-1301

Glitter Bay Hotel $-$$
Bajan-fine American.
Porters, ☎ 422-4111

Great Escape $
Bajan and Caribbean.
Belleville, St Michael,
☎ 436-3554

**Heywoods Restaurants
and Bars $$**
A wide range of options
from breakfast to fine
dining, Captains Table, El
Comedor, Caroline's
Restaurant and Beach
Ideal Restaurant $-$$
Bajan snacks. Cave
Shepherd, Broad Street,
Bridgetown, ☎ 431-2121

**Holetown Fish
and Chip $**
Seafood. Sunset

Ideal Restaurant $$
Open all day American,
snacks and deli. Top
Floor, Cave Shepherd,
Broad Street,
Bridgetown, ☎ 431-2139

Il Tempio $$-$$$
Italian. Fitts Village,
St James, ☎ 432-2057

Indigo $$
Seafood specialties plus
meat and vegetarian
dishes. Holetown,
☎ 432-2996

Jeff Mex $$
Mexican. Bridgetown,
☎ 431-0857

Kascades Restaurant $$
English-International.
Paynes Bay, ☎ 432-7981

Kitchen Korner $$
Local and International.
Holetown, ☎ 432-1684

Koko's Restaurant $$
Fine Bajan. Prospect,
☎ 432-1684

**La Cage aux
Folles $$-$$$**
International haute
cuisine. Summerland
Great House

Lone Star $$$
European and Caribbean
fine cuisine, reservations
recommended. The
Garden, St James,
☎ 419-0599

Laguna Restaurant $-$$
International. Colony
Club, ☎ 422-2335

La Maison $$-$$$
International Gourmet.
Holetown, ☎ 432-1156

La Terra $$-$$$
Italian, reservations
recommended. Baku
Beach, Holetown,
☎ 432-1099

**Le Chateau
Creole $$-$$$**
Cajun-French. Porters,
☎ 422-4116

Ly Jing Restaurant $$
Chinese. Broad Street,
Bridgetown

Legend Restaurant $-$$
Bajan. Mullins Bay,
☎ 422-0631

Mango's By The Sea $
Bajan specialities, great
lobster. Speightstown,
☎ 422-0704

Mayflower $-$$
Chinese. Bridgetown,
☎ 426-4734

The Mews $$
Seafood-International.
Holetown, ☎ 432-1122

**Min's Chinese
Restaurant $-$$**
Chinese. Holetown,
☎ 432-5481

**Mullins Beach Bar
and Restaurant $-$$**
Bajan fare. Mullins,
☎ 422-1878

Neptunes $$-$$$
Seafood. Tamarind Cove,
☎ 432-6999

**Next Door Wine
Bar and Bistro $-$$**
Bajan-Continental.
Paynes Bay, ☎ 432-5738

**Nico's Champagne
and Wine Bar $-$$**
Seafood-Bajan-French.
Holetown, ☎ 432-6386

Olive's Bar $$
Mediterranean-Caribbean. *Holetown,*
☎ 432-2112

Old Stables $-$$
Light lunches Mon to Fri.
*Tyrol Cot and Heritage
Village, Codrington Hill,*
☎ 425-777

Orchid Room $$$
International. *Colony
Club,* ☎ 422-2335

Patisserie Flindt $-$$
Desserts and pastries,
light lunches. *1st Street,
Holetown,* ☎ 432-2626

Peppers $$
Champagne bar-bistro.
Holetown, ☎ 432-7549

Putters on the Green $$
Local and International.
Sandy Lane, St James,
☎ 432-6557

Raffles Restaurant $-$$
Caribbean. *Holetown,*
☎ 432-6557

Ragamuffins $$
Caribbean. *Holetown,*
☎ 432-1295

Reflections $$
Crystal Cove, ☎ 432-2683

**Reid's Restaurant
$$-$$$**
Excellent elegant
International dining.
Derricks, ☎ 432-7623

The Restaurant $$
Caribbean and Oriental
fine dining, reservations
required. *Sandy Lane,*
☎ 432-2838

The Rose $$
Seafood and jazz.
Prospect, ☎ 425-1074

**Royal Pavilion
Hotel $$-$$$**
Caribbean-International.
Porters, ☎ 422-4444

Rumours $$
Bajan-International.
Palm Beach, Holetown,
☎ 432-5294

Rusty Pelican $$
American. *Bridge House,
Bridgetown,* ☎ 436-7778

Sakura $$-$$$
Creative Japanese and
sushi bar. *Holetown,*
☎ 432-5187

Sandpiper $$-$$$
Bajan and International
Gourmet cooking.
St James Beach,
☎ 422-2251

**Sandy Lane Golf Club
Restaurant, $$-$$$**
Caribbean-Oriental.
St James, ☎ 432-2838

Sandy's Restaurant $$
Bajan and International.
Sandridge Beach Hotel,
☎ 422-2361

Schooner $$
Seafood. *Grand Barbados
Beach Resort, Aquatic
Gap,* ☎ 436-8719

Settlers Beach $$-$$$
Bajan-International.
Settlers Beach Hotel,
☎ 422-3052

Sitar $$
East Indian. *2nd Street,
Holetown,* ☎ 432-2248

Smugglers Cove $$
Seafood-Bajan. *Paynes
Bay,* ☎ 432-1741

South Deck $$
Mediterranean-bistro
style. *The Boatyard,
Carlisle Bay,* ☎ 436-2622

Sundown $
Caribbean. *The Garden,
St James,* ☎ 422-0457

Surfside $$
Bajan & Caribbean.
Holetown, ☎ 432-2105

**Tamarind Cove
Hotel $$-$$$**
Bajan-seafood. *Paynes
Bay,* ☎ 432-1332

Tams Wok $$
Chinese. *Holetown,*
☎ 432-8000

The Townhouse $$-$$$
Caribbean haute cuisine.
Holetown, ☎ 422-2296

**Treasure Beach Hotel
$$-$$$**
Local and International
Gourmet. *Paynes Bay,*
☎ 432-1346

Waterfront Cafe $-$$
Nouvelle Bajan and
vegetarian. *The
Carenage, Bridgetown,*
☎ 427-0093

**Weisers On
The Bay $-$$**
Caribbean. *Brandons,
St Michael,* ☎ 425-6450

Zino's Diner $$
Creole-seafood-
vegetarian. *Bay Street,*
☎ 435-3053

South Coast

Angie's $-$$
Bajan-light meals.
*Sand Acres Beach Club,
Maxwell Coast Road,*
☎ 428-5380

Applessence $$
Bajan. *Hastings,*
☎ 436-7604

**Asta Hotel
Restaurant $$**
Bajan-seafood. *Hastings,*
☎ 427-2541

B4 Blues Restaurant $$
International.
St Lawrence Gap,
☎ 435-6560

Eating out on Barbados

Barbecue Barn $$
Bajan-American.
Rockley, ☎ 430-3402

Beachfront $$
Bajan-BBQ. *Worthing,*
☎ 435-8000

Bean 'n Bagel $-$$
Bagels, pastries, light
lunches. *St Lawrence
Gap,* ☎ 420-4604

Beijing $-$$
Chinese. *St Lawrence,*
☎ 435-6000

Bellini's $$
Italian. *St Lawrence Gap,*
☎ 435-7246

Bert's Bar $$
American, Bajan and
seafood. *Abbeville Hotel,
Worthing,* ☎ 435-8502

Blakey's $$
Local and International.
St Lawrence,
☎ 428-1933

Boomers $$
Local and International.
St Lawrence,
☎ 428-1511

Boucan $$-$$$
Gourmet dining with
entertainment and
Sunday jazz. *Savannah
Hotel, Hastings,*
☎ 228-3800

Bourbon Street $$
Cajun-Creole. *Prospect,
St James,* ☎ 424-4557

Bubba's Sports Bar
Kebabs, steaks and
seafood. *Hastings,*
☎ 436-6217

Café India $$
Excellent Indian.
St Lawrence Gap,
☎ 435-6531

Café Jungle $-$$
Grills, salads and
sandwiches. *Sheraton
Centre,* ☎ 437-1127

Cafe Sol $$
Mexican. *St Lawrence
Gap,* ☎ 435-9531

Captain's Carvery $-$$
Bajan buffet. *St
Lawrence,* ☎ 435-6961

Carib Beach Bar $$
Bajan-American.
Worthing, ☎ 435-8540

Casuarina $$
Bajan-International.
*Casuarina Beach Club,
St Lawrence Gap,*
☎ 428-3600

**Champers Wine Bar
and Restaurant $$**
Mediterranean/local,
Saturday night Dinner
and Floor Show.
Hastings, ☎ 435-6645

Charlie's $$
Local and International.
Worthing, ☎

Chefette $-$$
American-BBQ. *Oistins,*
☎ 428-2223 (and several
other locations)

Chicken Barn $-$$
Grill. *Worthing,*
☎ 435-7428

China Gardens $-$$
Chinese. *Maxwell Main
Road,* ☎ 428-8179

Cloud 9 Restaurant $$
Bajan-International. *Club
Rockley,* ☎ 435-7880

Courtyard $$-$$$
International.
Sunbury Great House,
☎ 423-6270

The Crane $$-$$$
Award winning seafood,
reservations requested.
Crane Bay, St Philip,
☎ 423-6220

Croton Bar and Deli $$
Great fish every Friday
and Saturday. *Maxwell
Main Road,* ☎ 428-7314

Da Luciano $$
International. *Hastings,*
☎ 427-5518

David's Place $$
Excellent Bajan.
St Lawrence, ☎ 435-9755

Deli Bistro $$
International. *Hastings,*
☎ 435-3354

Desmonds $-$$
Local. *City Centre,
Bridgetown,* ☎ 437-2218

Doreen's Kitchen $$
Bajan. *Worthing Court
Hotel,* ☎ 435-7910

Fat Andy's $$
Fun American Diner.
Hastings, ☎ 435-8121

Fishpot $$
Seafood. *Maxwell*

Frog and Gecko $$
Poolside dining, local
and International.
St Lawrence Gap,
☎ 435-6801

Fronds Restaurant $$
Organic food grown at
the Future Centre.
Edgehill, ☎ 425-2020

Garden Terrace $$-$$
Bajan-International.
*Southern Palms Beach
Club,* ☎ 428-7171

Guangong $$
Chinese. *Worthing,*
☎ 435-7387

Ile de France $$-$$$
French fine dining.
Holetown, ☎ 422-3245

Inn Place $-$$
Bajan. *Welcome Inn
Hotel, Maxwell Coast
Road,* ☎ 428-4833

IV Play Deli $-$$
Guyanese, Trinidad and
Creole. *Sheraton Centre,*
☎ 437-2099

Eating out on Barbados

Jade garden $$
Chinese. *St Lawrence Gap,*
☎ 428-2759

Jambalaya's $$
Caribbean, Bajan and entertainment.
St Lawrence Gap,
☎ 435-6581

Jeremiah's $$
Bistro. *Maxwell Coast Road, Christ Church,*
☎ 420-3080

Josef's $$-$$$
International-Swedish.
St Lawrence, $ 435-8248

Lanterns By The Sea $$-$$$
Caribbean. *Bougainvillea Beach Resort, Maxwell Coast Road,* ☎ 418-0990

L'Azure Restaurant $-$$
Caribbean-Mediterranean. *St Lawrence Gap,*
☎ 435-6560

Le Petit Flambe $$
Seafood. *Southern Palms Beach Club,* ☎ 428-7171

Limers Restaurant $-$$
Bajan-seafood.
St Lawrence Gap,
☎ 435-6554

Lucky Horseshoe $$
Steakhouse and bar.
Worthing Main Road,
☎ 435-5825

Luigi's $-$$
Italian. *St Lawrence Gap,*
☎ 428-9218

Masquerade $$
Seafood, pasta and Indian. *St Lawrence Gap,*
☎ 435-6134

McBride's Pub and Cookhouse $$
International, entertainment, very lively.
St Lawrence Gap,
☎ 435-6352

Melting Pot $-$$
Caribbean. *St Lawrence,*
☎ 428-3555

Mermaid $-$$
Bajan-International,
Maxwell Coast Road,
☎ 428-4116

Mervue House Restaurant $$
Swedish-International, in a 19th century historic house. *Marine Gardens,*
☎ 435-2888

Mile Tree $-$$
International-Bajan.
Dover Convention Centre, St Lawrence Gap,
☎ 420-5910

Oceanside $$
Seafood. *St Lawrence Gap,* ☎ 435-6950

Ocean View Restaurant $$-$$$
Excellent Bajan. *Ocean View Hotel, Hastings,*
☎ 427-7821

Pebble $$
Seafood. *Needham's Point,* ☎ 436-8399

Picasso's $-$$
French bakery and café.
Sheraton Centre,
☎ 437-7634

Pisces Restaurant $$
Seafood. *St Lawrence Gap,* ☎ 435-6564

Pizza Man Doc $-$$
Pizza. *St Lawrence,*
☎ 435-8618

Plantation Restaurant and Dinner Show $$
St Lawrence, ☎ 428-5048

Red Rooster $$
International. *Hastings,*
☎ 435-3354

Roti Hut $
Indian. *Worthing,*
☎ 435-7362

Round Rock $$
Bajan specialties. *Silver Sands, Christ Church,*
☎ 428-7500

Sand Dollar $$
Vegetarian and contemporary Caribbean.
Worthing, ☎ 435-6956

Sandy Bank Beach Bar and Restaurant $$
Seafood-homemade fare.
Sandy Bank, ☎ 435-6689

Sandy Beach Hotel Kolors Oceanside Restaurant $$
Seafood. *Worthing,*
☎ 435-8000

Schooner Restaurant $$
Seafood-Bajan. *Carlisle Bay,* 436-8719

Sea Rocks $$
Seafood. *Maxwell,*
☎ 428-6648

Secrets $-$$
Seafood. *Maxwell Coast Road,* ☎ 428-9525

Shakey's Pizza $
Pizza. *St Lawrence,*
☎ 420-777 (also in Hastings, ☎ 435-7777)

Ship Inn $-$$
Seafood-steaks-bar meals. *St Lawrence Gap,*
☎ 435-6961

The Shak $-$$
Bajan. *Dover Beach Hotel, St Lawrence Gap,*
☎ 428-8076

Shak Shak $$-$$$
Inspired Caribbean.
Hastings, ☎ 435-1234

Shakey's Restaurant $-$$
Bajan-pizza-snacks.
Hastings, ☎ 435-7777

Silver Rock $$
Seafood-International.
Silver Sands Beach,
☎ 428-2866

Southern Accents $$
Caribbean-South East Asia, *St Lawrence Gap*, ☎ 435-7246

Southern Palms $$
Bajan-International, *St Lawrence Gap*, ☎ 428-7171

Steak House $$
Seafood-steaks. *St Lawrence Gap*, ☎ 428-7152

St Lawrence Fishing Boat $$
Seafood-Caribbean. *St Lawrence Gap*, ☎ 435-7112

St Lawrence Pizza Hut $
Pizza. *St Lawrence*, ☎ 428-7152

Stowaways $-$$
Bajan-snacks. *Maxwell*, ☎ 420-6101

Sugar Reef Bay $$
International-Bajan. *Rockley*, ☎ 435-8074

Suzie Yong $$
Chinese. *St Lawrence*, ☎ 428-1865

Tamarind Tree Club $$
Bajan-seafood. *Hastings*, ☎ 427-4407

Tapps On The Bay $$
Seafood-American and entertainment. *St Lawrence Gap*, ☎ 435-7112

39 Steps $$
Bajan. Chattel Plaza, *Hastings*, ☎ 427-0715

Traitor's Gate $-$$
Seafood-Bajan-pub fare. *Maxwell Main Road*, ☎ 420-5204

Verandah $$-$$$
Seafood-Bajan. *Barbados Hilton, Aquatic Gap*, ☎ 426-0200

Virginian Restaurant $$
Bajan-International. *Hastings*, ☎ 427-7963

Water's Edge $$
Bajan and International. *Sand Acres Hotel, Maxwell Coast Road*, ☎ 428-2592

Whistling Frog $-$$
Pub food. *Time Out At The Gap, St Lawrence Gap*, ☎ 420-5021

Windsurfing Beach Club $-$$
Fast food-salads. *Maxwell Main Club*, ☎ 428-9095

Witch Doctor $-$$
Bajan. *St Lawrence Gap*, ☎ 435-6581

South-East and East Coast

Altantis $$
Seafood. *Bathsheba*, ☎ 433-9445

Bonito Bar and Restaurant
Bajan. *Bathsheba*, ☎ 433-9034

Chef's Table $$
Seafood and Continental. *Edgewater Inn*, ☎ 433-9900

Cliffside at Edgewater Inn $-$$
Bajan-International. *Bathsheba*, ☎ 433-9900

Coconut Inn $
Caribbean. *Sherbourne, St John*, ☎ 433-2697

Crane $$
Seafood. *Crane, St Philip*, ☎ 423-6220

Panoramic Restaurant $$
Bajan-Continental. *Crane Beach Hotel*, ☎ 423-6220

Peach and Quiet $$
Bajan-Seafood. *Inch Marlow*, ☎ 428-5682

Pot and Barrel $-$$
Bajan and International. *Long Bay*, ☎ 423-4107

Round House $$-$$$
Creative Bajan-International. *Bathsheba*, ☎ 433-9678

Rum Punch Bar and Restaurant $-$$
Burgers, chicken and seafood. *Barclays Park*, ☎ 422-9213

Sam Lord's Castle $$-$$$
Fabulous 7 course dinner. *Sam Lords Castle*, ☎ 423-7350

Silver Rock Restaurant $-$$
Bajan-seafood. *Silver Sands Beach*, ☎ 428-2866

Silver Sands $$
Bajan. *Silver Sands Hotel*, ☎ 428-6001

Struggles $-$$
International. *East Point, St Philip*, ☎ 423-0667

Sunbury Plantation House $-$$$
Bajan-English. *Sunbury Plantation*, ☎ 423-6270

ACCOMMODATION

There is a wide range of accommodation to suit all tastes and most pockets. There are luxury, all-inclusive resorts, convention hotels and specialist resorts offering diving, golf and tennis. All-inclusive resorts offer excellent value if you want to stay put, but if you want to get out and explore, look for accommodation offering room and breakfast, so that you can eat out at the many excellent island restaurants. There are also many luxury villas and cottages for rent, self-catering apartments and guest houses. Prices can vary enormously between high season (mid-December to mid-April) and the rest of the year. Many hotels have several tariffs.

There is a 5 per cent Government tax on hotel bills, and many establishments add a further 10-15 per cent service charge.

Prices are represented as $ inexpensive, $$ moderate and $$$ expensive.

Key: **AI** – All-Inclusive, **AP** – American Plan & Bed and all meals, **MAP** – Modified American Plan & bed, breakfast and dinner, **CP** – Continental Plan & bed and breakfast, **European** – Plan & bed only. **RR** – Rate on request. All hotels have restaurants and can arrange for fishing, diving, sailing and other recreational activities.

Villa Nova

Set in 14 acres (5.6 hectares) of tropical woodland, this former sugar plantation great house is now Barbados' first luxury Country House Hotel. There are 28 suites, 3 gourmet restaurants, games room, gym, pool, tennis, croquet, putting green, badminton and exclusive beach club (☎ 433-1524).

HOTELS

** All members of **Gems of Barbados**, a group of 3 and 4 star hotels offering a range of accommodation, locations and shared activities.

Christ Church

Abbeville $ EP
Accra Beach, Rockley
21 rooms, restaurant,
bar and pool, ☎ 435-7924

Accra Beach $$ EP
Rockley
128 rooms and suites, restaurants,
bar, gym, beach, pool,
☎ 435-8920

Asta $$ EP
Hastings
60 rooms, beach, kitchenette, pool,
deep sea fishing,
☎ 427-2541

Bagshot House RR
St Lawrence
16 rooms, beach, ☎ 435-6956

Blue Horizon Apartment Hotel $$ EP **
Rockley
120 one-bedroom apartments,
studio apartments and studios,
poolside restaurant, bar and
pools, ☎ 435-8916

Bougainvillea Beach Resort $$$ AI
Maxwell Coast Road, Christ Church
100 suites, with restaurants, pool,
bar, beach shop, beauty salon,
tennis, fitness center and business
center, ☎ 428-7141

Bresmay Apartment Hotel $$-$$$ EP
St Lawrence Gap
69 rooms, beach, kitchenette,
pool, ☎ 428-6131

Butterfly Beach $$ EP
Maxwell Coast Road
47 rooms, with kitchenettes,
restaurant, bar, beach, pool and
watersports, ☎ 428-9095

Caribbee $$ AI
Hastings
55 rooms, beach, kitchenette,
pool, ☎ 436-6232

Casuarina Beach Club $$$ EP
Dover
166 rooms, restaurant and bar,
beach, kitchenette, tennis, pools,
☎ 428-3600

The Club $ EP
Hastings
15 rooms, beach, kitchenette,
pool, ☎ 436-7604

Club Rockley Barbados $$$ AI
Rockley
107 rooms, beach, kitchenette,
pool, tennis and golf, ☎ 435-7880

Coconut Court Beach $ EP
Hastings
90 rooms, restaurant and bar,
beach, kitchenette, pool,
☎ 427-1655

Croton Inn $
Maxwell
6 rooms, ☎ 428-7314

Crystal Waters $ EP
Worthing
8 rooms, ☎ 435-7514

Divi Southwinds RR
St Lawrence
161 rooms, beach, kitchenette,
pool, ☎ 428-7181

Dover Beach $$ EP
St Lawrence Gap
39 rooms, restaurant and bar,
beach, kitchenette, pool,
☎ 428-8076

Dover Woods ER
St Lawrence Gap
4 rooms, ☎ 420-6599

Fairholme $ EP
Maxwell
31 rooms, beach,
kitchenette, restaurant,
pool, ☎ 428-9425

Golden Sands $$ EP
Maxwell
27 rooms, beach, kitchenette,
pool, ☎ 428-8051

Long Beach Club $ EP
Long Beach
24 rooms, restaurant and
bar, kitchenettes, shop,
beach, pool, ☎ 428-6890

Oasis $$-$$$ AI
Worthing
Kitchenette, restaurant
and bar, pool, ☎ 435-7930

Palm Garden $-$$ EP
Worthing
18 rooms, restaurant and bar,
kitchenette, pool, ☎ 435-6406

Peach and Quiet $-$$ EP
Inch Marlow
2 rooms, restaurant, bar,
beach, pool, ☎ 428-5682

PomMarine $$$
Hastings, Christ Church
Home of the Hospitality Institute of
the Barbados Community College,
restaurant and bar, ☎ 228-0900

Rainbow Reef $$ EP
Dover
43 rooms, restaurant and
bar, beach, pool and tennis,
☎ 428-5110

Regency Cove RR
Hastings
35 rooms, restaurant and bar,
kitchenette, pool, ☎ 435-8971

Riviera Beach Hotel $ EP
Rockley
40 rooms, kitchenette,
pool, ☎ 435-8970

Fact File

Sandy Beach Island Resort RR
Worthing
137 rooms, restaurant and bar, beach, pool and tennis, ☎ 435-8000

Savannah $$$ *
Hastings
101 rooms and suites, restaurant and bar, kitchenettes, pool, beach and conference facilities, ☎ 228-3800

Sea Breeze $$-$$$ EP
Maxwell Coast Road
60 rooms, beach, kitchenette and pools, ☎ 428-2825

Shells $
Worthing
7 rooms, ☎ 435-7253

Shonlan Airport Hotel $ EP
Coverley Terrace
16 rooms, kitchenette, ☎ 428-0039

Silver Rock $$$ AI *
Silver Sands
70 rooms, beach, kitchenette and pool with windsurfing school, scuba and watersports, ☎ 428-2866

Silver Sands $$-$$$ EP
Silver Sands
106 rooms, restaurant and bar, beach, kitchenette, pool and tennis, ☎ 428-6001

Southern Palms $$$ EP
St Lawrence Gap
92 rooms, beach, kitchenette, pools and tennis, ☎ 428-7171

Sunhaven Beach Apartment Hotel $-$$
Rockley, Christ Church, ☎ 435-8905

Time Out at the Gap $$ *
Dover Beach, St Lawrence Gap
76 rooms, pub, pool, restaurant, bar, gift shop and beach, ☎ 420-5021

Vacation Hotel $ EP
Enterprise
15 room, kitchenette, ☎ 428-4748

Welcome Inn AI
Maxwell
110 rooms, restaurant and bar, beach, sports, kitchenette, pool, ☎ 428-9900

Windsurf Beach $-$$
Maxwell
24 rooms, kitchenettes, bar, windsurfing center and beach, ☎ 420-5862

Woodville Beach $$
Hastings
36 rooms, kitchenettes, restaurant and bar, pool and beach, ☎ 435-6693

Worthing Court $-$$ EP *
Worthing
24 rooms and apartments, kitchenettes, restaurant and bar, pool, ☎ 435-7910

Yellow Bird $-$$ EP
St Lawrence Gap
19 rooms, kitchenettes, restaurant and bar, pool, ☎ 435-8444

St James

Almond Beach Club $$$ AI
Vauxhall
288 rooms, restaurant and bar, beach, pool, watersports, tennis and golf, ☎ 432-7840

Coconut Creek Club $$$ MAP
Derricks
53 rooms, beach, pool, ☎ 432-0803

Colony Club $$$ MAP
Porters
94 rooms, restaurant and bar, beach, pool, ☎ 422-2335

Coral Reef Club $$$ EP/MAP
Holetown
69 rooms, restaurant and bar, beach, kitchenette, pool, ☎ 422-2372

Crystal Cove $$$ MAP
Fitts Village
88 rooms, restaurant and
bar, beach, pool and tennis,
☎ 432-2683

Discovery Bay Beach $$$ MAP
Holetown
87 rooms, beach, pool
and tennis, ☎ 432-1301

Escape $$$ AI
Prospect
Restaurant and bar, pool, beach
and watersports, ☎ 424-7571

Glitter Bay $$$ EP
Porters
69 rooms, beach, kitchenette,
pools, watersports and tennis,
☎ 422-4111

Golden Palm $$$
Holetown
67 rooms, with pool, gift shop,
beach, tennis and golf, ☎ 432-666

Inn on the Beach $$-$$$ EP
Holetown
21 rooms, restaurant and bar,
beach, kitchenette, pool,
☎ 432-0385

Mango Bay $$$ AI
Holetown
64 rooms, restaurant and bar,
beach and pool, ☎ 432-1384

Regent St James $$$
Holetown
67 rooms, pool and beach,
☎ 432-6666

Royal Pavilion $$$ EP
Porters
75 rooms, restaurant and
bar, beach, pool and tennis,
☎ 422-5555

Sandpiper Inn $$$ EP
St James
45 rooms, restaurant and bar,
beach, kitchenette, pool and
tennis, ☎ 422-2251

Sandy Lane $$$
St James
Restaurant and bar,
health spa, ☎ 432-1311

Settlers Beach $$$ EP
St James
44 rooms, restaurant and bar,
beach, kitchenette, pool,
☎ 422-3052

Smugglers Cove $$ EP
Paynes Bay
21 rooms, beach, kitchenette,
pool, ☎ 432-1741

Sunset $$-$$$
Holetown
18 rooms, restaurant and bar,
kitchenettes, pool and beach,
☎ 432-2715

Tamarind Cove $$$ MAP
Paynes Bay
117 rooms, 3 restaurants and
bars, beach, pool and
watersports, ☎ 432-1332

Treasure Beach $$$ EP
Paynes Bay
25 rooms, restaurant and bar,
beach, pool, ☎ 432-1346

***Coconut Creek, Colony Club,
Crystal Cove and Tamarind Cove
are all members of the St James
Beach Hotel group. Guests have
access to most facilities at each
of the hotels.**

St Jospeh

Atlantis $ MAP
Bathsheba
8 rooms, beach, ☎ 433-9445

Edgewater Inn $ EP
Bathsheba
20 rooms, beach, ☎ 433-9900

Kingsley Club $$ EP
Cattle Wash
8 rooms, restaurant and bar,
beach, ☎ 433-9422

St Michael $$$ EP
Barbados Hilton, Aquatic Gap
184 rooms, restaurants and
bars, beach, pool and tennis,
☎ 426-0200

Grand Barbados Beach $$-$$$ EP
Aquatic Gap
133 rooms, beach, pool,
☎ 426-4000

Island Inn $$$ AI
Aquatic Gap
23 rooms, pool, ☎ 436-6393

Turtle Beach $$$ AI
Aquatic Gap
167 rooms, restaurants and
bars, pool, gift shop, gym, spa
and salon, pool, tennis and
watersports, ☎ 428-7131

St Peter $$$ AI
Almond Beach Village, St Peter
288 rooms, beach, pool, tennis
and golf, ☎ 432-7840

Cobblers Cove $$$ MAP/EP
Road View
39 rooms, beach, pool
and tennis, ☎ 422-2291

Kings Beach $$$ EP
Road View
57 rooms, restaurant and bar,
beach, pool, watersports and
tennis, ☎ 422-1690

Sandridge Resort $-$$ EP
St Peter
52 rooms, restaurant and bar,
beach, kitchenettes and pool,
☎ 422-2361

Sugar Cane Club $-$$EP
Maynards
20 rooms, kitchenette, pool,
☎ 422-5026

St Philip
Crane Beach $$$ EP
Crane
18 rooms, restaurant and bar,
beach, pool and tennis,
☎ 423-6220

Sam Lord's Castle $$$ EP
Long Bay
234 rooms,3 restaurants and bars,
beach, pool, watersports and
tennis, ☎ 423-7350

VILLAS FOR RENT

Alleyne, Aguilar and Altman	☎ 432-0840
Bajan Services	☎ 422-2618
Cottages, Gibbs Beach, St Peter, Barbados	☎ 422-2618
Realtors Limited	☎ 426-4900
Sunlink Realty	☎ 432-5396
Sunset Crest Resort	☎ 432-6666
or the Barbados Tourist Office	

AIRPORTS/AIRWAYS

Air Canada	☎ 428-5077
Air Martinique	☎ 431-1858
American Airlines	☎ 428-4170
BWIA	☎ 426-2111
Bajan Helicopters	☎ 431-0069
British Airways	☎ 428-0940/436-6413
Canadian	☎ 428-9324
Caribbean Airways	☎ 428-5660
Cruzeiro Brazilian Airlines	☎ 426-2111

LIAT	☎ 436-6224
Mustique Airways	☎ 428-1638
Trans Island Air	☎ 428-1654
Virgin Atlantic	☎ 418-8505

BANKS

Banks are open from 8am to 3pm Monday to Thursday, and from 8am to 1pm and 3pm to 5pm on Friday. They are not open at weekends and on pubic holidays. The airport bank is open from 8am to midnight daily. There are 24-hour ATM facilities at the Royal Bank of Canada and the airport and a growing number of locations around the island.

Bank of Nova Scotia
Broad Street, Bridgetown
☎ 431-3000

Barbados Development Bank
Central Bank Building, Bridgetown
☎ 436-8870

Barbados National Bank
Broad Street, Bridgetown
☎ 431-5700

Barclays Bank
Rendevouz, St Michael
☎ 431-5300

Central Bank of Barbados
Church Village, Bridgetown
☎ 436-6870

Royal Bank of Canada
Broad Street, Bridgetown
☎ 426-5200

BEACHES

The island boasts 70 miles (113km) of coastline and many spectacular beaches, all of which are public. Although some areas close to large hotels and resorts may be reserved for guests or there may be a charge to use facilities. Sand varies from pure white to pink, a result of millions of grains of crushed coral. Because of the surrounding coral reefs the waters around the island are generally calm. The sea is slightly rougher on the north and eastern sides because of the prevailing winds and the Atlantic breakers which have traveled all the way from the African coast, while the leeward side offers very safe swimming. Best beaches include:

West Coast

Brighton Beach – this long expanse of beach is very popular but be wary of sea urchins.

Mullins Beach – clear warm waters, refreshments and drinks available, snorkeling, shade and parking by the beach.

Sandy Lane – there is public access on either side of the hotel whose facilities can be used for a small charge. Refreshments, snorkeling and watersports available.

Paynes Bay – Large, easily accessible beach with refreshments, snorkeling and watersports.

Also Heywoods, Godings, Paradise, Brandon, Browne's and Greaves End Beaches.

South Coast

Accra and Rockley Beach – a very popular beach with adjacent roadside parking, refreshments, watersports, rental equipment, body surfing. A place to go to see and be seen.

Silver Sands Beach – safe swimming in the shallow lagoon, convenient parking, refreshments and lots of beach activities.

Casuarina Beach – large popular beach which attracts a breeze which produces slightly larger waves, so good for windsurfing. Refreshments are a fair walk away, so this is a good place to bring your own picnic.

Also Enterprise and Miami Beach, Needham's Point, and Sandy Beach.

South-East Coast

Foul Bay – park in the New Road car park. An area with big waves, some fishing boats and large expanses of near-deserted beach. Bring your own refreshments.

Crane Beach – the pink sand beach is backed by cliffs and dunes and the waves make it suitable for body surfing. Refreshments are available at the hotel.

Bottom Bay – Park on top of the cliff and use the steps to get to the beach with coconut palms and a cave to explore. The water color is splendid.

East and North Coast

Bath – one of the safest swimming beaches on the east coast.

Bathsheba area – there are huge stretches of beautiful beach with excellent surfing and the island's biggest waves. The waves are strong and there are undercurrents. Only strong, experienced swimmers should swim here.

Also Morgan Lewis Beach and Maycock's Beach.

BEAUTY PARLORS AND HEALTH CLUBS

Most of the major hotels and resorts have their own facilities and will take bookings from non-residents, and there are also a number of independent salons and health clubs.

BICYCLE RENTAL

There are several bicycle rental locations around the island. Rates are around $20 a day with discounts for longer rentals.

CAMPING

There are no public campgrounds on Barbados and as almost all the land is privately owned, camping is not allowed.

CAR RENTAL

To rent a car you must have a valid driver's license or an International license, and major credit card for security deposit. These allow you to purchase a temporary Barbados license which costs Bds$10. This can be obtained from the police desk at the airport, Hastings, Worthing and Holetown police stations, also the licensing authority offices in Oistins, Christ Church, the Pine in St Michael's, and Folkstone in St James, or through the car rental company. It is valid for one year.

Car rental costs from about Bsd$90 a day for a small manual car or from Bsd$130 for an automatic. Weekly rentals start from about Bds$400 a week for a small car, and from Bsd$650 a week for a large saloon. Rates include third party insurance, but not personal accident insurance or damage to the vehicle. There is a government tax of 12.5 per cent on all rentals. Always check the rental car before driving away. Check the condition of the tires, make sure there is a good spare and that the brakes are in good working order.

Cars drive on the left and the speed limit is 30mph (50kph) in towns and 40mph (60kph) on rural highways, and 50mph (80km) on signposted highways. Road distances are now generally given in kilometres. Service stations are open daily until about 7pm, although there are some open 24 hours a day and many only accept cash for fuel. Bajan drivers honk their horns a lot both to warn of their approach round dangerous corners, or simply to say hello to a passing friend. Avoid Barbados rush hours on weekdays between 7am and 8.30am and 4.30pm to 5.30pm.

Rental cars are recognized by an H on the number plate, and most locals take heed of this and accept any eccentricities in your driving – within reason. Once you get off the main roads, drive with care. There are pot holes, uneven road surfaces and in some places, hardly any road surface at all. There are also narrow roads, tight bends and frustrating signposting, which is why a good map of the island is essential.

Useful hint: When driving and not sure of your direction look for a) bus signs which tell you if you are travelling to or away from Bridgetown, and b) look for signs on buses. If a bus passes you on the other side of the road with a sign saying it is going where you plan to be, turn round and follow it.

If you are involved in an accident, leave the vehicle where it is and report it to the local police and the car rental company as quickly as possible. Write down the details of other drivers, how the accident happened, who was at fault and the names and addresses of any witnesses and, if possible, get the other parties to sign it.

In the event of a breakdown, contact the car rental company as quickly as possible for a replacement. At night, contact the police who can usually get in touch with the car rental company.

Car rental companies

Abbac Rentals	☎ 428-8149
ABN Rentals	☎ 432-0226
Access	☎ 427-0215
ACM Rentals	☎ 426-3169

Fact File

Adams Car Rentals	☎ 436-0543
AJ's Rentals	☎ 438-4545
Auto Rentals (Hertz)	☎ 428-1520
Belmont Taxi Service	☎ 429-2659
Burrowes Car Rentals	☎ 423-9052
Butcher	☎ 438-3529
Clarke Car Rentals	☎ 420-7766
Coconut Car Rentals	☎ 437-0297
Coral Isle	☎ 428-9000
Corbin's Car Rentals	☎ 427-9531
Country Rentals	☎ 429-1386
Courtesy Car Rentals	☎ 431-4160
Direct Rentals	☎ 428-2491/420-6372
Double J Car & Moke Rentals	☎ 427-3155
Drive-A-Matic	☎ 422-4000
Eastern Enterprises	☎ 435-4405
Express Rent A Car	☎ 428-7845
Exquisite Limousine Service	☎ 425-2643
Fat Jack's Moke and Car Rentals	☎ 420-6502
Frederick's	☎ 424-4322
Henry's Car Rentals	☎ 433-1270
Hill's Car Rentals	☎ 426-5280
Johnson Stables and Garage	☎ 426-5181
Jones Garage	☎ 426-5030
King Vere Transport Services	☎ 422-2459
Leisure Rentals	☎ 423-5377
M&C Moke	☎ 427-1952
M&R Rental	☎ 438-2399
MAH Car Rentals	☎ 427-1952
Mangera Car Rentals	☎ 436-0562
Mohammed Car Rentals	☎ 426-3073
Myles Garage and Car Rentals	☎ 420-5229
National Car Rentals	☎ 426-0603
P and S Car Rentals	☎ 424-2052
Paramount Taxi Service	☎ 429-3718
PK Enterprises	☎ 436-5895
Premier Auto Rentals	☎ 424-2277
Ray's Enterprises	☎ 436-3560
Rayside Car Rentals	☎ 428-0264
Regency	☎ 427-5663
Sealy's Car Rentals	☎ 429-4627
Selman's	☎ 438-2119
Smith LE and Co	☎ 436-5895
Stoute's Car Rentals	☎ 435-4456
Sunny Isle Motors	☎ 435-7979
Sunset Crest Rent-a-Car	☎ 432-1482 (St James)
	☎ 426-1763 (Christ Church)
Thompson William B Car and Moke	☎ 428-7500
Top Car	☎ 435-0378
Top Class	☎ 228-7368
Williams LE Tours	☎ 427-1043

Motor scooters

One and two-seater motor scooters can be rented by the day or the week. Weekly rental works out much cheaper and includes third party insurance. You will have to leave your credit card number as a security deposit, or up to Bsd$200 which is refundable when the scooter is returned as borrowed. A valid driver's license is required plus a temporary Barbados license that costs Bsd$10 (see car rental above). There are scooter rentals at Lynn's Rentals, Hastings, Christ Church (☎ 435-8585), and Fun Seekers, Rockley Main Road, Christ Church (☎ 435-8206).

CHURCHES

All the main religious denominations are represented. These include Anglican, African Methodist Epsicopal, Barbados Baptist Convention, Bahai Faith, Berean Bible Church, Christian Science, Church of Jesus Christ of the Latter Day Saints, Jehovah Witness, Jewish, Methodist, Moslem, Pentecostal Assemblies of the West Indies, Roman Catholic, Salvation Army, Seventh Day Adventists and the Worldwide Church of God.

Some useful numbers: St Michael's Cathedral (☎ 427-0790), St Patrick's Cathedral (☎ 426-2325).

CINEMAS/MOVIE THEATERS

There are three movie theaters on the island – **The Vista Cinema**, close to the junction of Worthing Road and Rendevouz Hill (☎ 435-8400), the **Globe Cinema**, Upper Roebuck Street, Bridgetown (☎ 426-4692) and the **Glove Drive-In** at Adams Castle, Christ Church (☎ 437-0479/0480).

CONFERENCE FACILITIES

The **Sherbourne Conference Centre** at Two Mile Hill, St Michael, is one of the top conference destinations in the Caribbean. Set in 5 acres (2 hectares) of tropical gardens, the modern facility can accommodate 1,200 delegates and has 25,000 sq ft (2,250 sq m) of exhibition space (☎ 434-3000). The **Sir Garfield Sobers Sports Complex** at Wildey, St Michael, can accommodate up to 4,000 people. Many hotels also have conference and meeting facilities.

CURRENCY AND CREDIT CARDS

The official currency is the Barbados dollar (Bds) which is tied to the US dollar, and US dollars are widely accepted. The Bds comes in bills of 2 (blue), 5 (green), 10 (brown), 20 (purple), 50 (orange) and 100 (gray) dollars. The official exchange rate for other currencies varies and it is best to exchange money at banks. You will generally get a less favorable exchange rate at exchange bureaus and hotels. As a rough guide reckon that US$1=Bds$2, and that £1=Bds$3, although obviously rates vary. There is a small service charge for converting foreign currency into

Barbados dollars, and a larger one for converting it back. You will need your passport to conduct a foreign currency transaction at a bank. ATM machines dispense only local currency. All major credit cards are accepted by hotels, restaurants, car rental companies and large shops. American Express is represented on the island by the Barbados International Travel Service, Horizon House, McGregor Street, Bridgetown (☎ 431-2400 or 931-2423).

CUSTOMS AND IMMIGRATION

For stays of less than three months proof of identification and an onward return ticket are required. US and Canadian citizens need either a valid passport, or an original or certified copy of their birth certificate, naturalization certificate or laminated picture ID, or US or Canadian voter registration card together with a photo driver's license. British and Commonwealth citizens require a valid passport with at least six months to run after the date of onward return journey. Visas may be necessary for nationals of other countries. Before you arrive you will be handed an immigration card that must be filled in and handed to the immigration officer. The card is stamped and must be retained during your stay and handed in on departure. After clearing immigration, collect your luggage and proceed through customs.

Visitors arriving in Barbados are allowed to bring in 200 cigarettes or 50 cigars or half a pound (0.2kg) of tobacco, and one liter of spirit or wine. The import of flowers, fruit and plants is restricted.

Departing US visitors are allowed to take up to US$400 of purchases, Canadian visitors are allowed to take back C$300 worth of goods a year. Japanese visitors are allowed to take home up to US$1700 worth of duty-free goods.

Departure Tax

There is a departure tax of Bds$25 (US$13).

ELECTRICITY

The electrical supply is generally 110 volts/50 cycles although some hotels also provide interchangeable 115/220 volt sockets. European appliances will need adapters, and some may be damaged by using a lower voltage.

EMBASSIES AND CONSULATES

Australian Embassy, Bishop's Court Hill, St Michael, ☎ 435-2834

Brazilian Embassy, Fairchild Street, Bridgetown, ☎ 427-1735

British High Commission, Collymore Rock, ☎ 436-6694

Canadian High Commission, Bishops Court Road, St Michael, ☎ 429-3550

Consulate of Belgium, Rockley, ☎ 435-7704

Commission of the European Community, Prince Alfred Street, Bridgetown, ☎ 427-4362

French Consul, Waverley House, Hastings, ☎ 435-6847
German Consul, Rosebuck Street, Bridgetown, ☎ 427-1876
Italian Vice-Consul, Bannatyne, Christ Church, ☎ 437-1228
Netherlands Consul, Balls Plantation, Christ Church, ☎ 418-8000
Norwegian Consul, Nile Street, Bridgetown, ☎ 429-7286
Swedish Consul, Fairchild Street, Bridgetown, ☎ 426-2482
USA Embassy, Bridgetown, ☎ 436-4950

EMERGENCY TELEPHONE NUMBERS

Police	☎ 112	**Ambulance**	☎ 115
Fire	☎ 113	**Coast Guard**	☎ 427-8819

GALLERIES

There are many wonderful galleries on the island. They include:
Art Foundry, Rum Factory and Heritage Park, ☎ 418-0714
Bagatelle, Bagatelle Great House, St Thomas, ☎ 421-6767
Barbados Gallery of Art, Garrison, St Michael
Barbados Museum, Garrison, St Michael, ☎ 436-1956
Bagatelle Art and Craft Gallery, Bagatelle, St Thomas, ☎ 421-6767
Barbados Arts Council, Pelican Village, Bridgetown, ☎ 426-4385
Earthworks Pottery, Edgehill, St Thomas, ☎ 425-0223
Gang of Four, Speightstown, ☎ 419-0051
Mango's Fine Art Gallery, Speightstown, ☎ 422-0704
Portobello Gallery, Batts Rock, St James, ☎ 424-1687
Potters House Gallery, Earthworks, ☎ 425-3463
Kirby Gallery, Courtyard Hastings, ☎ 430-3032 and
  Boatyard, Bay Street ☎ 430-3033
Verandah Art Gallery, Bridgetown ☎ 426-2605

HEALTH

There are no serious health problems although visitors should take precautions against the sun and biting insects such as sand flies and mosquitoes, both of which can ruin your holiday. Biting bugs tend to come out late in the afternoon. Other minor problem areas include one or two nasty species of wasps, and there are scorpions although these are very rare, and their sting is usually painful rather than dangerous. Be careful around fire coral and be alert for jelly fish and spiny black sea urchins, especially around coral, which are occasionally a problem at some times of the year. Immunization is not required unless travelling from an infected area.

Most hotels and resorts have doctors on call around the clock and emergency dental treatment is also available at all times.

Hospitals

The main hospital is the 600-bed **Queen Elizabeth's**, Lower Collymore Rock (☎ 436-6450), and there is also the private **Bayview Hospital**, St Paul's Avenue (☎ 436-5446). Both are on the outskirts of Bridgetown. There are almost a score of modern health centers and clinics throughout the island.

Tanning safely

The sun is very strong but sea breezes often disguise just how hot it is. If you are not used to the sun, take it carefully for the first two or three days, use a good sunscreen with a factor of 15 or higher, and do not sunbathe during the hottest parts of the day. Wear sunglasses and a sun hat. Sunglasses will protect you against the glare, especially strong on the beach, and sun hats will protect your head.

If you spend a lot of time swimming or scuba diving, take extra care, as you will burn even quicker because of the combination of salt water and sun. Calamine lotion and preparations containing aloe are both useful in combating sunburn.

Irritating insects

Mosquitoes, midges and sand flies can be a problem almost anywhere. In your room, burn mosquito coils or use one of the many electrical plug-in devices that burn an insect repelling tablet. Mosquitoes are not so much of a problem on or near the beaches because of onshore winds, but they may well bite you as you enjoy an open-air evening meal. Use a good insect repellant, especially if you are planning trips inland such as walking in the rain forests. Fire ants are also found in wooded areas, and their bites can be very irritating. Bay rum essences can be soothing.

Sand flies can be a problem on the beach. Despite their tiny size they can give you a nasty bite. Ants abound, so make sure you check the ground carefully before sitting down otherwise you might get bitten, and the bites can itch for days.

Note: Drinking water from the tap is perfectly safe although bottled mineral and distilled water is widely available.

INSURANCE

Make sure you have adequate insurance to cover all eventualities. Health care, if required, is expensive, and if hiring a car it is worth taking out extra insurance such as damage collision waiver. If you have rented a car as part of a package deal, check what insurance cover this includes and make up any shortcomings.

LANGUAGE

The official language is English, but a local patois, a combination of old English and West African languages, is widely spoken. The patois is virtually incomprehensible to visitors. It also takes a little time to get used to the everyday island English. As the slaves had to pick up the new language from the plantation overseers and owners, many of the terms used today reflect the style of English spoken in England in the 17th and 18th century. In fact, some of the street dialogue one hears could have come straight from the pen of Shakespeare. Married women, for instance, are still called Mistress rather than the contraction missis used today. The 'th' sound does not exist so the word 'that' is pronounced 'dat', and 'the' is 'de'. Other speech has strong elements of Welsh, Scottish and particularly, West Country. Many words and phrases commonly used today, result from mishearings centuries ago, for instance, hue and cry is now human cry, and many words derive from West African dialects, like duppy, a West African Twi tribal word for ghost, or a wandering spirit, and bassa-bassa, which means talking nonsense. The African custom of doubling up some nouns is common, with words like boy child, rock stone and she cow.

Adjectives are often used twice or repeated three times to give added emphasis i.e. a fast car is fast, but if it is fast, fast, it really motors. And if your hosts say they are tired, tired, tired, it is time to excuse yourself and leave!

Words worth knowing are: cool out (relax), bad (good), real bad (very good), jump up (impromptu party), chat down (to flirt) and tie-goat (a married person). If you ask directions it can be confusing if you are told to: 'go so, then above, then below'. You are actually being directed to go straight on (go so) then turn right (above), then left (below).

There are hundreds of colorful expressions such as break five, meaning to shake hands, and hold strain, which means don't get so agitated, and many wonderfully practical proverbs.

A favorite saying is 'de higher de monkey climb, de more'e show'e tail'. This is the equivalent of 'the bigger you are, the harder you fall', meaning the more important you become and the higher you climb, the more exposed you are to public scrutiny, and the further it is to fall if you come crashing down.

Another saying is 'to fire a few grogs' which means to have a drink or two, and it has an historical origin. In 1731 Admiral Vernon ordered that rum served to Royal Navy sailors in the West Indies fleet be diluted to reduce drunkenness and indiscipline. The Admiral had a habit of striding about the deck wrapped in a grogram cloak, and was called Old Grog, and so the watered-down rum was named Grog, a name that is still used today. And, the saying: 'de new broom sweep cleaner but de ole broom know de corners', needs no translation. There are some wonderful books on the Bajan dialect, proverbs and folklore in local stores.

MEDIA

The two daily newspapers are the tabloids *Advocate* and *Nation* that are more entertaining than informative, and both have sensational Sunday editions. *The Broad Street Journal* is a weekly business publication. The *Caribbean Contact* is published monthly and is full of interesting news and information. Most major US newspapers and many foreign papers and magazines are readily available although always at several times their normal price. The Caribbean Broadcasting Corporation broadcasts the local television channel while some US networks, such as CNN, are

also available via satellite. There are a number of island radio stations mostly offering music.

NIGHTLIFE

There is an enormous choice of nightlife and evening entertainment from English pubs to Bajan rum shops, and late nightclubs to classical concerts. Most large hotels and resorts offer dinner cabarets, like **Club Xanadu** at the Ocean View Hotel, or live evening entertainment, usually featuring island musicians, singers and dancers. You can dine like a queen at Marriott's Sam Lord's Castle which every Wednesday offers the same sumptuous eight-course dinner served to Queen Elizabeth when she visited Barbados, or enjoy a beach-barbecue to the accompaniment of steel band. At the **Sherbourne Center** you can enjoy a dinner buffet and '1627 and all that', an evening of folk dance, music and drama which relates the history of the island (☎ 429-6016). The **Barbados Museum** stages a fun murder mystery show over buffet dinner, and **The Tropical Spectacular Dinner Show**, at the Plantation Restaurant (☎ 428-5048), is rated as one of the best dinner shows in town. In Bridgetown there are clubs where you can listen to local bands, jazz or folk, or disco dance. The most popular clubs attract thousands of dancers on Friday and Saturday nights, and some stay open all night. Local dances are held frequently and widely advertised. Night cruises with music, dancing and quite a lot of rum are also popular.

Lively nightspots

South coast

After Dark, St Lawrence Gap	☎ 435-6547
B4 Blues Restaurant and Bar, St Lawrence Gap	☎ 435-6560
Carib Beach Bay, Worthing	☎ 435-8540
Club Needhams, Hilton Hotel	☎ 428-3333
Club Xanadu, Ocean View Hotel, Hastings	☎ 427-7821
Fisherman's Wharf, Bridgetown	☎ 436-7778
Harbour Lights, Bridgetown	☎ 436-7225
Jambalaya's, St Lawrence Gap	☎ 435-6581
Limers Bar and Restaurant, St Lawrence Gap	☎ 435-6554
McBrides, St Lawrence Gap	☎ 435-6352
Reggae Lounge, St Lawrence Gap	☎ 435-6462
Rusty Pelican, The Carenage, Bridgetown	☎ 436-7778
Ship Inn, St Lawrence Gap	☎ 435-6961
Sandy Bank Beach Bar and Restaurant, Hastings	☎ 435-6689
StowAways, Maxwell	☎ 420-6101
Sugar Reef Bar and Restaurant, Rockley	☎ 435-8074
Thirty Nine Steps Wine Bar, Hastings	☎ 427-0715

| **Warehouse**, Bridgetown | ☎ 436-2897 |
| **Waterfront Café**, Bridgetown | ☎ 427-0093 |

West coast

Bamboo Beach Bar, Paynes Bay	☎ 432-0910
Casbah, Holetown	☎ 432-2258
Club Milki, Heywoods Resort	☎ 422-4900
Coach House, Paynes Bay	☎ 432-1163
Cricketers' Pub, Coconut Creek Hotel	☎ 432-0803
Fathoms, Paynes Bay	☎ 432-2568
Hippo Disco, Barbados Beach Village	☎ 425-1440
Nico's Champagne and Wine Bar, Holetown	☎ 432-6386
Rumours Bay, Holetown	☎ 432-5294
Mullins Beach Bar and Restaurant, Mullins Beach	☎ 422-1878

PETS

There are strict rules about bringing in pets because of the rabies-free state of the island. Permits and rules of entry can be obtained from the **Ministry of Agriculture**, Graeme Hall, Christ Church (☎ 428-4150).

PHOTOGRAPHY

The intensity of the sun can play havoc with your films, especially if photographing near water or white sand. Compensate for the brightness otherwise your photographs will come out over-exposed and wishy-washy, especially if you take pictures when the sun is at its strongest. A low speed film is preferable – ASA 64 for slides, or ASA 100 for prints and underwater shots. If photographing on the beach in bright sunlight set the camera at least one stop and perhaps two below the reading from the built in light meter. The heat can actually damage film so store reels in a box or bag in the hotel fridge if there is one. Also remember to protect your camera if on the beach, as a single grain of sand is all it takes to jam your camera, and if left unprotected, it might 'disappear'. Film is expensive and it is best to bring your own, but if you have to buy, make sure it still has a good shelf life. It is also a good idea to bring with you any replacement batteries your camera might need.

It is very easy to get 'click happy' in the Caribbean, but be tactful when taking photographs. Many islanders are shy or simply fed up with being photographed, and some might insist on a small payment. You will have to decide whether the picture is worth it, but if a person declines to have their photograph taken, don't ignore this. The islanders are a warm and very hospitable people, and if you stop and spend some time finding out what they are doing, they will usually then allow you to take a photograph.

POST

The main post office is next to **Cheapside Market** on the outskirts of Bridgetown. It is open from 7am to 5pm Monday to Friday. It also has a philatelic bureau (☎ 436-4800), and there are post offices in every parish open from 8am to noon and 1pm to 3.15pm (3pm on Monday). Stamps are sold in many stores, hotels and attractions. Postcards to the US and Canada require a 65c stamp, postcards to Europe need a 70c stamp.

PUBLIC HOLIDAYS* AND MAJOR EVENTS

January
1 January – New Year's Day *

February
Holetown Festival

March
Ash Wednesday *

April
Good Friday *
Easter Monday *

May
1 May – May Day *

July
Crop Over Festival

August
Crop Over Festival

November
National Independence
Festival of Creative Arts
30 November – Independence Day

December
December 25 – Christmas Day *
December 26 – Boxing Day *

SECURITY

Barbados has a low crime rate and the overwhelming majority of the islanders are friendly and scrupulously honest. However, with so many tourists about there are temptations so sensible precautions should be taken to avoid trouble. It makes sense like anywhere else, not to walk around wearing expensive jewelry or flashing large sums of money. If out late at night, travel by taxi or with a crowd, and don't stray into unfamiliar, badly lit areas. It is a good idea to get a street map and familiarize yourself with it, learning the best way back to your hotel. Don't leave valuable items in unattended vehicles, or on the beach if going swimming, and lock doors at night.

Don't carry around your passport, travelers checks or all your money. Keep them secure in your room or in a hotel safety deposit box. It is also a good idea to have photocopies of the information page of your passport, your air ticket and holiday insurance policy. All will help greatly if the originals are lost. Most hotels have their own security staff, but care should also be taken with valuables when by the pool and on the beach.

As with most tourist destinations, you might be pestered by touts trying to sell tours, souvenirs and even drugs. A firm 'no' or 'not interested', is normally enough to persuade them to leave you alone.

Women are likely to be pestered by Bajan 'beach boys' even if they have a male escort in tow. It is part of a long-standing ritual, but if you do not seek attention, say no firmly but politely from the start.

SHOPPING

Most shops are open from 8am to 4pm but supermarkets stay open longer. Saturday is early closing for many stores which close at 12.30pm. Shops and boutiques of all kinds can be found on the island selling a huge range of goods. There are duty-free shops and designer boutiques, crafts markets and top-name salons, as well as street vendors and roadside stands, and remember that haggling over the price is all part of the fun. Best buys include island arts and crafts such as pottery, costume dolls, woodwork and woodcarving, weaving, batik, shell and coral jewelry, paintings by local artists, tapes of local musicians and Bajan rum. Barbados stamps, available from the bureau at the General Post Office, also make colorful and interesting souvenirs.

Broad Street is the main shopping district in Bridgetown. It has a wide range of stores close together, with the added advantage that most have air-conditioning. There are also lots of places to eat and get a drink, if you plan to spend all day shopping. Of interest is the **Norman Shopping Centre**, tax-free **Da Costa's Mall** and **Cave Shepherd**, the largest and most chic department store in the Caribbean. In the store you can enjoy a rum punch in the Balcony Cafe, or traditional Bajan cooking in the Ideal Restaurant.

Places outside Bridgetown to shop include the tax-free shops in the departure lounge of the **Grantley Adams Airport**, the **Sheraton Centre** at Sergeant's Village, inland from St Lawrence Gap, with 75 shops, boutiques and restaurants, the boutiques in most of the major hotels, and the shopping centers in Holetown, Speightstown, Hastings, Worthing and Oistins. All also offer a choice of restaurants and rum shops.

If you are interested in antiques you must visit **Greenwich House Antiques** in the old plantation house at Trents Hill, Greenwich Village (☎ 432-1169). The great house, outhouses and showroom are packed with thousands of pieces of old Barbadian furniture, silver, china, porcelain, pictures, prints, maps, jewelry, and lots more. It is open daily from 10.30am to 6pm, and worth a visit just to browse.

Caribbean Classic cards offer discounts at more than 1,000 outlets in Barbados and many other Caribbean islands. They cost US$10 and are valid for one year from September to August, and give discounts in participating restaurants, shops, watersports and dive operations, car rental, photo services, night clubs and so on (☎ 427-5046).

SIGHTSEEING AND CRUISES

There are many companies offering sightseeing and specialist tours. There are tours of the island by land, sea and air, and many tours are offered to the surrounding islands, especially Grenada, St Lucia, St Vincent and the Grenadines.

Fact File

Island tour companies

Adventureland	☎ 429-3687
Atlantis Submarines	☎ 436-8929
Bajan Helicopters	☎ 431-0069
Bajan Rep Services	☎ 428-7449
Bajan Holidays	☎ 438-4043
Barbados National Trust	☎ 426-4241
Boyce's Tours	☎ 425-5366
Calypso Tours	☎ 420-8028
Caribbean Safari Tours	☎ 427-5100
Custom Tours	☎ 425-0099
Highland Outdoor Tours	☎ 438-8069
Island Safaris	☎ 429-5337
Johnson's Stables	☎ 426-4205
St James Travel and Tours	☎ 432-0774
Thomas Weir Travel and Tours	☎ 437-6040
VIP Tours	☎ 429-4617

Cruises

The Jolly Roger Pirate Cruise – enjoy a day sailing cruise up the west coast, party atmosphere, Barbados barbecue-style lunch anchored off Holetown, a swim or laze on the beach and lots of music and rum punch.

There are also evening cruises from Bridgetown Harbour aboard the **Bajan Queen Mississippi**-style boat with Bajan dinner and disco (☎ 436-6424). **Calypso Cruises** aboard the *Irish Mist* catamaran with live Calypso, drinks, buffet and snorkeling equipment (☎ 436-9201), **Stiletto Catamaran Cruises** (☎ 231-3829/230-3495), **Tiami and Wind Warrior Sailing Cruises** for lunch and sunset cruises and private charters (☎ 425-5800), and **Secret Love Sailing Cruises** for all day and snorkeling cruises (☎ 437-7490.) **Harbour Master Cruises** also offer full day and dining and entertainment cruises (☎ 430-0900).

SPORTS

Cricket is the national game and played with such a fervor that it is not surprising that the West Indies are world champions. Barbados has produced an impressive array of world class players such as Sir Garfield (Gary) Sobers, Wes Hall, Evertton Weekes, Clyde Walcott and Sir Frank Worrell, the first black captain of the West Indies team, and many, many others.

The game is played at every opportunity and anywhere. You can be driving in the countryside, turn a corner, and confront players using the road as a wicket. It is played on the beach using a strip of palm for a bat, and even in the water if the tide is coming in. If the island team or the West Indies are playing, almost all the radios on the island are tuned in for the commentary, and matches at the Kensington Oval always draw capacity crowds and a festive atmosphere with picnics. The Kensington Oval is one of the four international test grounds in the Caribbean.

Many of the top Barbados Cricket League and Association clubs have been playing for more than 100 years. And, when cricket is not being played, football (soccer) is the top sport, with hockey, softball and volleyball also popular.

Hockey is played year round because of the good weather, but the local season runs from the end of May to November. The annual Banks Beer International Hockey Festival regularly attracts men's and women's teams from Europe, North and South America and the Caribbean.

The Barbados Volleyball Association was founded in 1976, and both the men's and women's national teams are Caribbean champions. Both dominoes and draughts have huge followings, a reminder of British involvement and the fact that many households do not own a television set. The French game of boule is also popular and played throughout the island, as is outdoor shuffleboard.

Race walking has grown enormously in popularity in recent years, and international events attract impressive fields. Local races also attract large numbers of young and old people. The largest of these is held at the Garrison Savannah, starts around 6am and involves 35 laps of the sand track. The walking is even tougher because it is on sand, but is a great way of getting fit.

For the visitor, there is a huge range of sporting opportunities from swimming and scuba diving, to horseback riding and hiking, to golf and tennis. There is cycling, sailing, squash and, of course, fishing either from shore or boat. Most hotels offer a variety of sports and water activities, and there are diving schools where you can learn what it is all about and progress to advanced level if you have the time.

Walking is great fun and there are lots of trails, especially in the mountains, but have stout, non-slip footwear and a waterproof. Protect yourself against insects, carry adequate drinking water and keep an eye on the time, because night falls quickly and you don't want to be caught out on the trail after dark. Guides can be arranged to escort you on these walks and make sure you get the most out of your trip.

Cycling

Bikes are available for rent at a number of resorts and bike rental companies. These include: **Fun Seekers**, Rockley Main Road, Christ Church (☎ 435-8206), **Williams Bicycle Rentals**, Hastings, Christ Church (☎ 427-3955), and **Irie Mountain Bikes**, Prospect (☎ 424-4730).

Rentals start from about Bsd$17 a day, mountain bikes are more expensive. Check to see if third party insurance is included. A security deposit is usually required.

Deep sea fishing

There is excellent deep sea fishing for world-record beating fish. The best fishing is generally found off the north and south coasts where the currents are strongest. Catches include albacore, dorado (known locally as dolphin), wahoo, blue and white marlin, yellowfin tuna, snapper, mackerel, barracuda, snook, tarpon and sailfish. Local records include

Fact File

blue marlin 505lbs (227 kg), yellow fin tuna 167.5lbs (75 kg), sailfish 78.25lbs (35 kg), wahoo 74lbs (33 kg) and dolphin 50lbs (22 kg).

Most hotels and resorts offer fishing trips and there are many charter boats available. Independent charters include: **Barracuda Too** (☎ 426-7252), **Blue Marlin Charters** (☎ 436-4322), **Blue Jay** (☎ 422-2098), **Barracuda Too** (☎ 426-7252), **Cannon Charters** (☎ 424-6107), **Challenge Tiami Sailing Cruises** (☎ 436-5725), **Honey Bea 3** (☎ 428-5344), **Jolly Roger Watersports** (☎ 432-7090), **Southern Palms** (☎ 428-7171).

Diving

The waters off Barbados offer world class diving. They are clear and teem with marine life. There are dives to suit all levels of experience, ranging from shallow reefs and caverns to trenches, deep walls and drop-offs. The waters are warm with year-round temperatures averaging between 80 and 90°F (26 and 32°C), and wet suits are not needed for warmth. The reefs are host to large numbers of tropical fish and a wide range of marine plants and animals. There are sea horses, angel fish, grunts, puffer fish, parrot fish, filefish, squirrel fish, barracudas, stingrays, eels, large spiny lobsters and green turtles. Coral formations include barrel, vase, tube sponges, sea fans, deep-water gorgon and black coral. Do not touch or damage the coral and avoid sea urchins, and fire coral. Both snorkelers and scuba divers should use a marker buoy if some way off shore to alert boats. The best snorkeling is in the calm, clear waters off the west coast. **Carlisle Bay** is one of the most popular dive sites because of the large number of wrecks.

There are several licensed diving centers offering equipment rental and full training. These include:

Bubbles Galore, The Boatyard, Bay Street	☎ 430-0354
Carib Ocean Divers	☎ 422-4414
Coral Isle Divers	☎ 434-8377
Dive Boat Safari	☎ 427-4350
Dive Hightide, Aquatic Gap	☎ 426-9947
Exploresub Barbados	☎ 435-6542
Hightide Watersports, Sandy Lane Hotel	☎ 432-0931
Scuba Rogers Shack	☎ 436-3483
Scuba Barbados	☎ 435-6565
Underwater Barbados, Carlisle Bay Centre	☎ 426-0655
West Side Scuba Centre, Baku Beach, Holetown	☎ 432-2558

For those who prefer to snorkel there are also many opportunities, and you do not need to have your own equipment as it can be rented, and it is provided free on some day tours. **Ocean Rebel Cruises** (☎ 428-7192) offer snorkeling trips.

Shipwrecks

There are a number of wrecks around the coast, some the victims of the reefs, and others deliberately sunk to create artificial reefs. Since 1666 it is estimated that more than 200 ships have foundered off shore, mostly during hurricanes and severe storms. In 1694 a hurricane sank 26 merchants ships in Carlisle Bay with the loss of more than 1,000 lives. Wrecks that can be explored include the 62-foot (19m) French tug which sank in 1919 in just 21 feet (6m) of water, the 120-foot (37m) long schooner, the *Fox* which sits in 43 feet (13m) of water and famous as the home of 'Hot Lips' an inquisitive Moray eel, and the *Sea Trek*, which was deliberately sunk in 1985 close to the *Fox* to create a marine habitat. The *SS Stavronokkita*, a 365-foot (111m) Greek freighter, was gutted by fire and the wreck bought by the Barbados Government who sank it in 1976 to create an artificial reef. It is in 137 feet (42m) of water, with the surface only 18 feet (5m) above the top of the rigging, and the home of George, the 'dancing' barracuda.

Popular dive sites

Barge Wreck – 20 feet (6m), an easy first wreck dive.

Bell Buoy – 30 to 60 feet (10 to 20m), lots of ledges and channels in the coral.

Berwin Wreck – 20 to 40 feet (6 to 12m), teeming with fish in Carlisle Bay.

Bright Ledge – 65 to 130 feet (20 to 40m) explore coral mountains.

Clarkes Reef – 40 to 130 feet (12 to 40m), a huge coral area.

The Dottings – 30 to 50 feet (9 to 15m), a flat coral area sometimes frequented by sharks.

Fisherman's Reef – 40 to 60 feet (12 to 20m) a reef teeming with fish.

Heywoods Reef – 20 to 60 feet (6 to 20m) good snorkelling.

Lord Cumbermere Wreck – 30 to 50 feet (9 to 15m) a 70-foot (21m) wreck lying on the coral reef.

Maycox Reef – 50 to 90 feet (15 to 27m) one of the island's most beautiful reefs in Maycox Bay.

Pamir Wreck – 60 feet (20m) the wreck of a 170-foot (52m) freighter.

The Pier – 20 to 40 feet (6 to 12m) a place to spot unusual species like frog fish and arrow crabs.

Silver Bank – 40 to 130 feet (12 to 40m) a large reef area teeming with fish.

Speightstown Reef – 30 to 50 feet (9 to 15m), a pretty coral reef.

Golf

Golf is a relative newcomer to the island, presumably because so much of the land was devoted to agriculture. The first 9-hole course was opened in 1946 at the **Rockley Resort Hotel** (☎ 435-7873), and later redesigned with an 18-hole course.

The island's newest course is the 18-hole, 6,870 yard (6282 m) championship **Royal Westmoreland**, designed by Robert Trent Jones Jr, with another 9 holes on the 480-acre (192 hectare) property (☎ 422-4653). There is also an 18-hole championship course at the **Sandy Lane Golf Club** (☎ 432-1311) just outside Bridgetown, and 9-hole courses at the **Rockley Golf Course** (☎ 435-7873), and **Almond Beach Village** (☎ 422-4900). There is also the 9-hole pitch and putt course at **Bel Air** (☎ 423-4653).

Gyms and health centers

Most of the top hotels have their own facilities. Others include:

Aquarion Body Club, Washington House, Bay Street, ☎ 436-2555

COB Fitness Centre, Speedbird House, Trafalgar Square, Bridgetown, ☎ 429-9287

Lady C's Day Spa, Rhondda Gardens, Rockley, ☎ 436-3464
Superior Fitness Gym, Speightstown Mall, ☎ 422-072
Surfside Health Club at the Hilton, Needham's Point, ☎ 436-1024
West One Studio, Dacostas West Mall, Sunset Crest, ☎ 432-5760
Winner Fitness Club, Wareners Building, Six Roads, ☎ 432-8466
World Gym Fitness Centre, Haggatt Hall, St Michael, ☎ 228-3319
Sir Garfield Sobers Sports Complex, Wildey, St Micahel, ☎ 437-6010

Horseback riding

Riding is available in all resort areas, and there are some wonderful scenic trails and beach rides. **Caribbean International Riding Centre** (☎ 433-1453), **Highland Outdoor Tours** (☎ 438-8069).

Horse racing and polo

Polo is still played at the **Barbados Polo Club** in St James and the Brighton Stables. There is racing at the **Garrison Savannah** on alternative Saturdays from January to March and May to October (☎ 432-1802).

Jet skis

Jet skis are available for hire from a number of locations, especially on the west coast. The ride is more exciting through the larger waves on the south coast. Jet skis are fun, but they can also be dangerous both for the rider and particularly other water users. Always be on the look out for, and make a wide berth of other people in the water.

Jogging and running

The resort areas have jogging trails or tracks, and road running is very popular. The **Run Barbados International Road Race** is held each December and attracts an international field. The event is in two parts, a full marathon and a 6 mile (10km) run in and around Bridgetown.

Motor racing and rally driving

Events are held at the **Bushy Park circuit** throughout the year.

Paragliding

Paragliding is allowed off **Hackleton Cliff**.

Squash

There are a number of courts around the island, principally at the **Barbados Squash Club** (☎ 427-7913), **Rockley Resort Hotel** (☎ 435-7880), **Casuarina Beach Club**, and **Heywoods Resort** (☎ 422-4900).

Surfing and windsurfing

The best surfing, both board and body, is off the east coast where the Atlantic breakers come ashore. Average on-shore winds are 10 to 20 knots. **Accra Beach** is a good place to learn, and **Crane Beach** is the place to show how good you are. **Bathsheba's Soup Bowl**, so called because of the foaming water, is the venue for national and international events. Boards are not readily available for hire, but a number of retailers sell them. There is para-sailing and excellent windsurfing, especially in **Little Bay** to the east of South Point, and along the stretch of north-east coastline between **The Choyce** and **The Chase**. You can hire windsurfing equipment at many oceanfront hotels and on some public beaches. The **Barbados Windsurfing Club** is based at Maxwell and Silver Sands, on either side of South Point.

Swimming

There are 70 miles (113km) of magnificent beaches and there are public beaches in all resort areas. The safest swimming is off the more sheltered west coast and care needs to be exercised in many of the waters off the east and south-east coast.

Tennis

Many of the large hotels and resorts have courts, and several offer floodlit tennis. If you are new to the island, book courts for early in the day or late in the afternoon so that you do not play when the sun is at its strongest.

Walking

There are a number of trails, mostly along the coast, and from January to March, the National Trust arrange conducted rural walks, usually about 3 miles (5km). These early morning Sunday walks often attract 2-300 walkers so are a great way of meeting like-minded souls. The walkers are then split into 'ability' groups so that if you want to go fast or slow, you will be with others travelling at the same pace. When out walking, always wear sturdy, non-slip shoes, wear a hat and carry an adequate amount of drinking water. When walking in high temperatures, you need to drink more liquid and take frequent rests.

Water skiing

The best water skiing is off the calm west coast and the best times are early morning or late in the afternoon when the waters are less crowded.

Yachting

The island's offshore waters attract yachts from around the world and there are a number of major races and regattas. The main event is the Atlantic Rally for Cruisers, a trans-Atlantic race from Gran Canaria with Barbados as the finishing point. There is also the annual Mount Gay Regatta which takes place in December. The best sailing is off the west and south coasts, and boats can be hired – bare-board or crewed. Many hotels and watersports centers have 10-foot (3m) sunfish, and 16-foot (5m) Hobie Cat catamarans.

Charter companies

Blue Jay Charters	☎ 423-4901
Cool Runnings	☎ 436-0911
Excellence	☎ 436-6424
Free Spirit	☎ 426-0890
Harbour Master Cruises	☎ 430-0900

Heat Wave	☎ 423-7871
Irish Mist	☎ 436-9201
Limbo Lady	☎ 420-5418
Regent One	☎ 421-6767
Rubaiyat	☎ 435-9913
Secret Love	☎ 432-1972
Stiletto Catamaran Cruises	☎ 231-3829/230-3495
Small Cats	☎ 421-6419
Tiami Cat Cruises	☎ 430-0900

TAXES

A 15 per cent VAT (Value Added Tax) is levied on most goods and services, including accommodation and restaurants.

TAXIS

Taxis generally do not have meters and most prices are fixed. However, it is important to agree a fare before setting off, and to know in which currency you are paying. Up to five people can travel in a taxi for the same price.

TELEPHONES AND COMMUNICATIONS

The telephone service is efficient, with direct international dialing from hotel rooms and lots of pay phones. The service is operated by the Barbados Telephone Company (Bartel) and Barbados External Telecommunications (BET). Local calls from pay phones cost 25c for five minutes and you insert the money when you hear the dial tone. Local calls are usually free when dialed from your hotel room. Phone cards are readily available and are convenient if you plan to make a lot of long-distance or international calls. Collect (reverse charge) calls can be made from public phones. The international dialing code for Barbados is 246, and from the US it is a long distance call – dial 1-246 and then the 7-digit US number. From the UK, dial 001-246 and then the local number. It is cheaper to make international calls at weekends and between 11pm and 7am weekdays.

TIME

Barbados is on Atlantic Standard Time, the same as New York, and five hours behind GMT, so when it is noon in London it is 7am in Bridgetown. Daylight Savings Time is not observed.

TIPPING

It is customary to tip about 10-15 per cent in restaurants and add the same to taxi fares. Some hotels and restaurants add a 15 per cent service charge to bills, so check to ensure you do not pay twice. Tip porters about $1 for each large piece of luggage carried, and leave room maids about $1 for each night's accommodation.

TOURIST OFFICES

Bridgetown Harbour
☎ 427-2623/800-744-6244,
email help@barbados.org

**Grantley Adams
International Airport**
Christ Church ☎ 428-7107/5570

Offices Abroad

USA

3440 Wilshire Boulevard, Suite
1207, Los Angeles CA 90010
☎ 213-380-2198

150 Alahambra Circle Suite 1270,
Coral Gables Fl 33134
☎ 305-442-7471

800 Second Avenue,2nd floor,
New York NY10017
☎ 212- 986-6516

Canada

Suite 1010, 105 Adelaide St West,
Toronto, Ontario M5H 1P9
☎ 416-214-9880

UK

263 Tottenham Court Road,
London W1P 9AA
☎ 020-7-636-9448

Germany

Neuve Mainer Strasse 22, 60311
Frankfurt a Main 1
☎ 069-24-26-96-30

WEDDINGS

Many people choose to marry in Barbados and it is now big business
with hotels having their own wedding consultants to help with all the
arrangements and a choice of venues for the ceremony from luxury
yachts to wedding gazebos on the beach. New laws make it even easier
to marry on the island, and you can wed the day you arrive if you
choose. In order to obtain a marriage license from the Ministry of Home
Affairs in Barbados, English or certified translations of the following
documents must be presented:
• Valid passports or birth certificates
• Proof that previous marriages ended in divorce or with the death of
  the spouse
• Letter from the authorized officiant who will perform the service
• Bsd$150 (US$75) if neither party is a Barbadian resident, and Bsd$25
  for the Revenue Stamp which can be obtained at any post office.

Roman Catholics wishing to marry need to satisfy a number of other
requirements, and details can be obtained from the office of the Bishop
of Bridgetown, St Patrick's Presbytery, PO Box 1223, Jemmott's Lane,
Bridgetown, Barbados (☎ (809) 426-3510).

WEIGHTS AND MEASURES

For a country with its roots so firmly tied with England, it is perhaps a
surprise to find that the metric system is used in a number of areas. Milk
and fuel is sold in liters, and road distances and speeds are given in
kilometers. Car speedometers usually indicate speed in both kilometers
and miles per hour.

INDEX

LANDMARK
VISITORS GUIDES

US & British VI*
ISBN: 1 901522 03 2
256pp,
UK £11.95 US $15.95

Antigua & Barbuda*
ISBN: 1 901522 02 4
96pp,
UK £5.95 US $12.95

Bermuda*
ISBN: 1 901522 07 5
160pp,
UK £7.95 US $12.95

Cayman Islands*
ISBN: 1 901522 33 4
144pp,
UK £6.95 US $12.95

St Lucia*
ISBN: 1 901522 82 2
144pp,
UK £6.95 US $13.95

Pack
2 months
into
2 weeks
with your
Landmark
Visitors
Guides

Jamaica*
ISBN: 1 901522 31 8
144pp
UK £6.95 US $12.95

Orlando*
ISBN: 1 901522 22 9
256pp,
UK £9.95 US $15.95

Florida: Gulf Coast*
ISBN: 1 901522 01 6
160pp
UK £7.95 US $12.95

Florida: The Keys*
ISBN: 1 901522 21 0
160pp,
UK £7.95 US $12.95

Dominican Republic*
ISBN: 1 901522 08 3
160pp,
UK £7.95 US $12.95

Gran Canaria*
ISBN: 1 901522 19 9
160pp
UK £7.95 US $12.95

Tenerife
ISBN: 1 901522 17 2
160pp,
UK £7.95

North Cyprus
ISBN: 1 901522 51 2
192pp
UK £8.95

Madeira
ISBN: 1 901522 42 3
192pp,
UK £8.95

   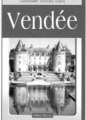 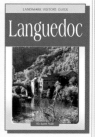

  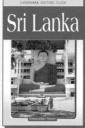  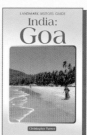

Published in the UK by
Landmark Publishing Ltd,
Waterloo House, 12 Compton, Ashbourne, Derbyshire DE6 1DA England
Tel: (01335) 347349 Fax: (01335) 347303
e-mail: sales@landmarkpublishing.co.uk
website: landmarkpublishing.co.uk

Published in the USA by
Hunter Publishing Inc,
130 Campus Drive, Edison NJ 08818
Tel: (732) 225 1900, (800) 255 0343 Fax: (732) 417 0482
website: www.hunterpublishing.com

ISBN 1 901 522 32 6
© **Don Philpott**

British Library Cataloguing in Publication Data: a catalogue record for this
book is available from the British Library.

Print: Gutenberg Press Ltd, Malta
Cartography:
Design: Samantha Witham

Front cover: Boats on Beach, St James Beach Hotels
Back cover, top: Enjoying a coctail at one Barbados' luxury hotels
Back cover, bottom: Bridgetown

Picture Credits
All photography supplied by the author except the following:
St James Beach Hotels, Barbados: Front cover, back cover top, 15T, 27,
34B, 43, 51B, 67,